DECREATION

DECREATION

Poetry, Essays, Opera

ANNE CARSON

VINTAGE CANADA

Unless otherwise noted, all translations are by the author.

VINTAGE   CANADA   EDITION,   2006

Copyright © 2005 Anne Carson

Published in Canada by Vintage Canada, a division of Random House of Canada Limited,
Toronto, in 2006, and simultaneously in the United States by Vintage Books, a division of Random
House, Inc., New York. Originally published in hardcover by Alfred A. Knopf,
a division of Random House Inc., New York, in 2005. Distributed by
Random House of Canada Limited, Toronto.

Vintage Canada and colophon are registered trademarks of
Random House of Canada Limited.

www.randomhouse.ca

Owing to limitations of space, permission to reprint previously published
material may be found at the end of the book.

Library and Archives Canada Cataloguing in Publication

Carson, Anne, 1950–
Decreation : opera, essays, poetry / Anne Carson.

ISBN-13: 978-0-676-97861-2
ISBN-10: 0-676-97861-4

I. Title.

PS8555.A7718D43 2006   C818'.54   C2006-902103-1

Manufactured in the United States of America.

2   4   6   8   9   7   5   3   1

for my students

"I love a poetical kinde of a march, by friskes, skips and jumps."

—Florio's 1603 translation of Montaigne's
"Essay on Some Verses of Virgil"

CONTENTS

ILLUSTRATIONS

S T O P S

SLEEPCHAINS

Who can sleep when she—
hundreds of miles away I feel that vast breath
fan her restless decks.
Cicatrice by cicatrice
all the links
rattle once.
Here we go mother on the shipless ocean.
Pity us, pity the ocean, here we go.

SUNDAY

My washed rags flap on a serious grey sunset.
Suppertime, a colder wind.
Leaves huddle a bit.
Kitchen lights come on.
Little spongy mysteries of evening begin to nick open.
Time to call mother.
Let it ring.
Six.
Seven.
Eight—she
lifts the receiver, waits.
Down the hollow distances are they fieldmice that scamper so drily.

LINES

While talking to my mother I neaten things. Spines of books by the phone.
Paperclips

in a china dish. Fragments of eraser that dot the desk. She speaks
longingly

of death. I begin tilting all the paperclips in the other direction.
Out

the window snow is falling straight down in lines. To my mother,
love

of my life, I describe what I had for brunch. The lines are falling
faster

now. Fate has put little weights on the ends (to speed us up) I
want

to tell her—sign of God's pity. She *won't keep me*
she says, she

won't run up my bill. Miracles slip past us. The
paperclips

are immortally aligned. God's pity! How long
will

it feel like burning, said the child trying to be
kind.

OUR FORTUNE

In a house at dusk a mother's final lesson
ruins the west and seals up all that trade.
Look in the windows at night you will see people standing.
That's us, we had an excuse to be inside.
Day came, we cut the fruit (we cut
the tree). Now we're out.
Here is a debt
paid.

NO PORT NOW

In the ancient struggle of breath against death, one more sleep given.
We took an offer on the house.
In the sum of the parts
where are the parts?
Silently (there) leaves and windows wait.
Our empty clothesline cuts the sloping night.
And making their lament for a lost apparel of celestial light
angels and detritus call out as they flow past our still latched gate.

WOULD BE HER 50TH WEDDING ANNIVERSARY TODAY

Cold orates upon a Roman wall.
Light is extreme (caught)
and shadows wait like
hoods to drop.
Brain taps
twice
for salt.

Was it Ovid who said, There is so much wind here stones go blank.

SOME AFTERNOONS SHE DOES NOT PICK UP THE PHONE

It is February. Ice is general. One notices different degrees of ice.
Its colours—blue white brown greyblack silver—vary.
Some ice has core bits of gravel or shadows inside.
Some is smooth as a flank, you cannot stand on it.
Standing on it the wind goes thin, to shreds.
All we wished for, shreds.
The little ones cannot stand on it.
Not one letter, not one stroke of a letter, can stand.
Blindingly—what came through the world there—burns.
It is February. Ice is general. One notices different degrees of ice.

THAT STRENGTH

That strength, mother: dug out. Hammered, chained,
blacked, cracked, weeping, sweeping, tossed on its
groans, hammered, hammering snouts
off death. Bolted and damming,
dolloped and biting. Knife. Un-
bloodable on grindbones
that strength, mother,
stopped.

METHINKS THE POOR TOWN HAS BEEN TROUBLED TOO LONG

Light on brick walls and a north wind whipping the branches black.
Shadow draws the gut of the light out dry against its palm.
Eat your soup, mother, wherever you are in your mind.
Winter noon is on the rise. Weak suns yet alive
are as virtue to suns of that other day.
For the poor town dreams
of surrender, mother
never untender,
mother gallant
and gay.

DESPITE HER PAIN, ANOTHER DAY

River fogs (7 AM) stray and begin, shiver and begin
on the September mill rocks.
Bits of leaf mirror along. I have arrived at my sanity.
Evidence (7 PM): while she medicates I walk by the river.
Millwheel smells like wet cornhusk.
On my back (2.38 AM) in the dark at Dorset Motel I listen to the radiator click
and to her, awake on the other side of town
in the hot small room
gripping a glow-in-the-dark rosary.
Whatever they say about time, life only moves in one direction,
that's a fact, mirroring along.
River fogs (7 AM) go flayed and silvery
when it dawns dark
on the day I leave.
DANGER DO NOT DROP OR DRAG ANCHOR
reads a sign just off the selvedges.
Mindingness gulps us.
Her on the bed as bent twigs.
Me, as ever, gone.

NOTHING FOR IT

Your glassy wind breaks on a shoutless shore and stirs around the rose.
Lo how
before a great snow,
before the gliding emptiness of the night coming on us,
our lanterns throw
shapes of old companions
and
a cold pause after.
What knife skinned off
that hour.
Sank the buoys.
Blows on what was our house.
Nothing for it just row.

Going to visit my mother is like starting in on a piece by Beckett.
              You know that sense of sinking through crust,
the low black *oh no* of the little room
with walls too close, so knowable.
Clink and slow fade of toys that belong in memory
          but wrongly appear here, vagrant and suffocated

                                    on a page of pain.
                              Worse
                              she says when I ask,
          even as (was it April?) some high humour grazes her eye—
      "we went out rowing on Lake Como"
  not quite reaching the lip.
              Our love, *that halfmad firebrand,*
                  races once around the room
                          whipping everything
                                  and hides again.

14

Hegel on sacrifice. The animal dies. The man becomes alert.
What do we learn we learn to notice everything now.
We learn to say he is a hero let him do it.
O is shown moving to the window.
What a rustling what an evening. *Oh little actor*
(living moving mourning lamenting and howling incessantly)
time to fly back to where they keep your skin.
Frail was it.
Sound of oars drawing away from shore.
That tang of dogshit in darkness.
That's your starry crown.
Off with his hood.

BECKETT'S THEORY OF COMEDY

Picking gooseberries, she said.
O is shown moving to the window.
Should traps be not available.
Or they kneel throughout the play.
That lifelong adorer!
Same old coat.
No verticals, all scattered and lying.
Tomorrow noon?
Goes back up the path, no sign of you.

[Pause.]

EVERY EXIT IS AN ENTRANCE

(A Praise of Sleep)

I want to make a praise of sleep. Not as a practitioner—I admit I have never been what is called "a good sleeper" and perhaps we can return later to that curious concept—but as a reader. There is so much sleep to read, there are so many ways to read it. In Aristotle's view, sleep requires a "daimonic but not a divine" kind of reading.[1] Kant refers to sleep's content as "involuntary poetry in a healthy state."[2] Keats wrote a "Sonnet to Sleep," invoking its powers against the analytic of the day:

> O soft embalmer of the still midnight!
> . . .
> Then save me, or the passed day will shine
> Upon my pillow, breeding many woes;
> Save me from curious conscience, that still lords
> Its strength for darkness, burrowing like a mole;
> Turn the key deftly in the oiled wards,
> And seal the hushed casket of my soul.[3]

My intention in this essay is to burrow like a mole in different ways of reading sleep, different kinds of readers of sleep, both those who are saved, healthy, daimonic, good sleepers and those who are not. Keats ascribes to sleep an embalming action. This means two things: that sleep does soothe and perfume our nights; that sleep can belie the stench of death inborn in us. Both actions are salvific in Keats' view. Both deserve (I think) to be praised.

My earliest memory is of a dream. It was in the house where we lived when I was three or four years of age. I dreamed I was asleep in the house in an upper room.

That I awoke and came downstairs and stood in the living room. The lights were on in the living room, although it was hushed and empty. The usual dark green sofa and chairs stood along the usual pale green walls. It was the same old living room as ever, I knew it well, nothing was out of place. And yet it was utterly, certainly, different. Inside its usual appearance the living room was as changed as if it had gone mad.

Later in life, when I was learning to reckon with my father, who was afflicted with and eventually died of dementia, this dream recovered itself to me, I think because it seemed to bespeak the situation of looking at a well-known face, whose appearance is exactly as it should be in every feature and detail, except that it is also, somehow, deeply and glowingly, strange.

The dream of the green living room was my first experience of such strangeness and I find it as uncanny today as I did when I was three. But there was no concept of madness or dementia available to me at that time. So, as far as I can recall, I explained the dream to myself by saying that I had caught the living room sleeping. I had entered it from the sleep side. And it took me years to recognize, or even to frame a question about, why I found this entrance into strangeness so supremely consoling. For despite the spookiness, inexplicability and later tragic reference of the green living room, it was and remains for me a consolation to think of it lying there, sunk in its greenness, breathing its own order, answerable to no one, apparently penetrable everywhere and yet so perfectly disguised in all the propaganda of its own waking life as to become in a true sense something *incognito* at the heart of our sleeping house.

It is in these terms that I wish to praise sleep, as a glimpse of something *incognito*. Both words are important. *Incognito* means "unrecognized, hidden, unknown." Something means not nothing. What is *incognito* hides from us because it has something worth hiding, or so we judge. As an example of this judgment I shall cite for you two stanzas of Elizabeth Bishop's poem "The Man-Moth." The Man-Moth, she says, is a creature who lives most of the time underground but pays occasional visits to the surface of the earth, where he attempts to scale the faces of the buildings and reach the moon, for he understands the moon to be a hole at the top of the sky through which he may escape. Failing to attain the moon each time he falls back and returns to the pale subways of his underground existence. Here is the poem's third stanza:

> Up the façades,
> his shadow dragging like a photographer's cloth behind him,
> he climbs fearfully, thinking that this time he will manage
> to push his small head through that round clean opening
> and be forced through, as from a tube, in black scrolls on the light.
> (Man, standing below him, has no such illusions).
> But what the Man-Moth fears most he must do, although
> he fails, of course, and falls back scared but quite unhurt.[4]

The Man-Moth is not sleeping, nor is he a dream, but he may represent sleep itself—an action of sleep, sliding up the facades of the world at night on his weird quest. He harbours a secret content, valuable content, which is difficult to extract even if you catch him. Here is the poem's final stanza:

> If you catch him,
> hold up a flashlight to his eye. It's all dark pupil,
> an entire night itself, whose haired horizon tightens
> as he stares back, and closes up the eye. Then from the lids
> one tear, his only possession, like the bee's sting, slips.
> Slyly he palms it, and if you're not paying attention
> he'll swallow it. However, if you watch, he'll hand it over,
> cool as from underground springs and pure enough to drink.

To drink the tear of sleep, to detach the prefix "un-" from its canniness and from its underground purposes, has been the project of many technologies and therapies—from the ancient temple of Asklepios at Epidauros, where sick people slept the night in order to dream their own cure, to the psychoanalytic algebras of Jacques Lacan, who understands sleep as a space from which the sleeper can travel in two directions, both of them a kind of waking. If I were to praise either of these methods of healing I would do so on grounds of their hopefulness. Both Asklepiadic priests and Lacanian analysts posit a continuity between the realms of waking and sleeping, whereby a bit of something *incognito* may cross over from night to day and change the life of the sleeper. Here is an ancient account of one of the sleep cures at Epidauros:

> There came as a suppliant to the god Asklepios a man who was so one-eyed that on the left he had only lids, there was nothing, just emptiness. People in the temple laughed at him for thinking he would see with an eye that was not there. But in a vision that appeared to him as he slept, the god seemed to boil some medicine and, drawing apart the lids, poured it in. When day came the man went out, seeing with both eyes.[5]

What could be more hopeful than this story of an empty eye filled with seeing as it sleeps? An analyst of the Lacanian sort might say that the one-eyed man has chosen to travel all the way in the direction of his dream and so awakes to a reality more real than the waking world. He dove into the nothingness of his eye and is awakened by too much light. Lacan would praise sleep as a blindness, which nonetheless looks back at us. What does sleep see when it looks back at us? This is a question entertained by Virginia Woolf in *To the Lighthouse*, a novel that falls asleep for twenty-five pages in the middle. The story has three parts. Parts I and III concern the planning and execution of a trip to the lighthouse by the Ramsay family. Part II is told entirely from the sleep side. It is called "Time Passes." It begins as a night that grows into many nights then turns into seasons and years. During this time, changes flow over the house of the story and penetrate the lives of the characters while they sleep. These changes are glimpsed as if from underneath; Virginia Woolf's main narrative is a catalogue of silent bedrooms, motionless chests of drawers, apples left on the dining room table, the wind prying at a window blind, moonlight gliding on floorboards. Down across these phenomena come facts from the waking world, like swimmers stroking by on a night lake. The facts are brief, drastic and enclosed in square brackets. For example:

[Mr. Ramsay, stumbling along a passage one dark morning, stretched his arms out, but Mrs. Ramsay having died rather suddenly the night before, his arms, though stretched out, remained empty.]

or:

[A shell exploded. Twenty or thirty young men were blown up in France, among them Andrew Ramsay, whose death, mercifully, was instantaneous.]

or:

[Mr. Carmichael brought out a volume of poems that spring, which had an unexpected success. The war, people said, had revived their interest in poetry.][6]

These square brackets convey surprising information about the Ramsays and their friends, yet they float past the narrative like the muffled shock of a sound heard while sleeping. No one wakes up. Night plunges on, absorbed in its own events. There is no exchange between night and its captives, no tampering with eyelids, no drinking the tear of sleep. Viewed from the sleep side, an empty eye socket is just a fact about a person, not a wish to be fulfilled, not a therapeutic challenge. Virginia Woolf offers us, through sleep, a glimpse of a kind of emptiness that interests her. It is the emptiness of things before we make use of them, a glimpse of reality prior to its efficacy. Some of her characters also search for this glimpse while they are awake. Lily Briscoe, who is a painter in *To the Lighthouse*, stands before her canvas and ponders how "to get hold of that very jar on the nerves, the thing itself before it has been made anything."[7] In a famous passage of her diaries, Virginia Woolf agrees with the aspiration:

> If I could catch the feeling I would: the feeling of the singing of the real world, as one is driven by loneliness and silence from the habitable world.[8]

What would the singing of the real world sound like? What would the thing itself look like? Such questions are entertained by her character Bernard, at the end of *The Waves:*

> "So now, taking upon me the mystery of things, I could go like a spy without leaving this place, without stirring from my chair. . . . The birds sing in chorus; the house is whitened; the sleeper stretches; gradually all is astir. Light floods the room and drives shadow beyond shadow to where they hang in folds inscrutable. What does this central shadow hold? Something? Nothing? I do not know. . . ."[9]

Throughout her fiction Virginia Woolf likes to finger the border between nothing and something. Sleepers are ideal agents of this work. So in her first novel, *The Voyage Out* (a story in which Clarissa Dalloway and six other people travel to South America on a boat), she places her heroine in a remarkable paragraph afloat between waking and sleep:

"I often wonder," Clarissa mused in bed, over the little white volume of Pascal which went with her everywhere, "whether it is really good for a woman to live with a man who is morally her superior, as Richard is mine. It makes one so dependent. I suppose I feel for him what my mother and women of her generation felt for Christ. It just shows that one can't do without *something*." She then fell into sleep, which was as usual extremely sound and refreshing, but visited by fantastic dreams of great Greek letters stalking round the room, when she woke up and laughed to herself, remembering where she was and that the Greek letters were real people, lying asleep not many yards away. . . . The dreams were not confined to her indeed, but went from one brain to another. They all dreamt of each other that night, as was natural, considering how thin the partitions were between them and how strangely they had been lifted off the earth to sit next each other in mid ocean. . . .[10]

I think Virginia Woolf intends us to enjoy the gentle marital experiment in which Clarissa condenses her husband (Richard) with Christ and then Christ with *something*—put in italics to remind us of its proximity to *nothing*. But I am not sure how "natural" it is for dreams to go stalking from brain to brain on an ocean liner, or for ancient Greek letters of the alphabet to be identified with real people. Something supernatural is beginning to be conjured here. Slightly more spooky is a story Virginia Woolf published in 1921 called "A Haunted House," which features a pair of ghosts sliding from room to room of a house where they had lived centuries ago. The ghosts seem happy but their transit through the house is disturbing, not least of all in its pronouns. The narrative voice shifts from "we" to "one" to "you" to "they" to "I," as if no one in the story can keep a stable skin on, and the story ends with a sleeper startled awake by the ghosts leaning over her bed:

Waking, I cry "Oh, is this *your* buried treasure? The light in the heart."[11]

I don't exactly know what the last two sentences mean. A transaction of some importance seems about to take place. Between the realms of sleep and waking, life and death, Virginia Woolf throws open a possibility of dispossession, and then leaves it standing ajar, as if she isn't sure which side she wants to be on. The story, although light and almost comical, leaves a dark aftertaste. Let us compare the supernatural effects of an earlier author. Homer locates the psychological climax of the *Iliad* in a scene at the start of the twenty-third book where Achilles falls asleep and is visited by the *psyche* of his dead friend Patroklos. Achilles converses with Patroklos and vainly tries to embrace him. As he reaches out his arms in sleep towards his dead friend, Achilles may remind us of poor Mr. Ramsay in *To the Lighthouse,* stretching out his arms in square brackets to his dead wife. Yet Homer's metaphysic of sleep is much less dark than Virginia Woolf's. Ghosts in epic are sad but they are also efficacious. While Patroklos goes gibbering off to his place in the underworld, Achilles jumps out of bed to perform the funeral rites enjoined on him by the dream, with this careful comment:

> "Soul and ghost are certainly *something!*"[12]

Sleepers in Virginia Woolf do not negotiate sublime transactions in this way. Her narrative advises us to place no hope in them:

> ... and should any sleeper, fancying that he might find on the beach an answer to his doubts, a sharer of his solitude, throw off his bedclothes and go down by himself to walk on the sand, no image with semblance of serving and divine promptitude comes readily to hand bringing the night to order and making the world reflect the compass of his soul. ... Useless in such confusion to ask the night those questions as to what

26

and why and wherefore, which tempt the sleeper from his bed to seek an answer.[13]

In Homer on the other hand, we find answers, beds and sleepers often intertwined, especially in the *Odyssey*. You could say the *Odyssey* is a saga of who sleeps with whom, in its driving mythic impulse towards Penelope and away from Helen, in its fantastic elaboration of kinds of beds, culminating in the famous "trick of the bed" whereby Penelope and Odysseus prove who they are. Throughout the poem, Homer orchestrates a master sleep plan that pulls all the major characters into a nocturnal rhythm lying just under the surface of the awake narrative. Let's look more closely at how people sleep and where their beds are in this epic.

Telemachos, to begin with, is an insomniac. On the seven occasions in the *Odyssey* when we observe him going to bed, only once does he "take the gift of sleep" in Homer's phrase. Usually he lies awake worrying, as at the close of Book 1:

> There all night long, wrapped in a sheep fleece,
> he deliberated in his mind the road Athene had shown him.[14]

or at the beginning of Book 15:

> Sweet sleep did not get hold of Telemachos but in his heart
> throughout the ambrosial night, cares for his father kept him awake.[15]

Cares for his father include, not least of all, cares for who his father is. When Athene asks him if he is Odysseus' son he gives a tough teenage answer:

> Well my mother says I'm his but I'm dubious
> myself: no one ever knows his own begetting.[16]

Yet he would certainly like to know. Sexual knowledge ripples everywhere in this story just out of Telemachos' reach. He sits amid the suitors "biting his heart" as they cavort before his mother. He travels to the houses of other married couples, Nestor and his wife, Menelaos and Helen, where he passes the night on a couch aligned with the marital bed. Thus pursued by primal scenes and primary doubts he makes his way to the sixteenth book and to the hut of Eumaios, the swineherd, where he finally meets and knows his father. Here Telemachos "takes the gift of sleep," lying down in the swineherd's hut beside Odysseus. This idyllic, impossible night as substitute Penelope beside his own father is Telemachos' happiest moment in the *Odyssey*. The very next evening sees him returned to his childhood and to insomnia: back at Penelope's house, as Odysseus plans the rout of the suitors, he sends Telemachos upstairs to bed alone:

> Then there Telemachos laid himself down
> and waited for radiant dawn.[17]

Meanwhile Odysseus: no question the man of many turns is a master of waking reality, yet his relation to sleep is troubled. He frequently feels the need to force himself awake, as when predatory animals or rapacious humans surround him (5.473; 8.445), or because a roomful of eager listeners wants to hear one more chapter of his adventures (11.379). Whenever he does nod off, catastrophes occur. Sailing from the island of Aiolos, whose king has given him a bag containing all the winds, Odysseus dozes on deck and his companions get curious:

> "So they loosened the bag and the winds all rushed out together.
> Storm winds seized them and carried them wailing their hearts out,
> over the sea away from their homes. But I
> awakened from sleep, considered in my excellent heart

whether to drop from the deck and die right there in the sea
or to endure, keep silent, go on being one of the living."[18]

Odysseus has another suicidal moment occasioned by sleep, in Book 12 when slumber overtakes him on the beach of Thrinakia and his companions slaughter the cattle of the sun. Odysseus wakes up and cries out:

"O father Zeus and you other gods who live forever,
how to my ruin you have lulled me in pitiless slumber!"[19]

So let's say in general Odysseus and sleep are not friends. Whatever this may mean for the hero's characterization overall, I'm struck by how Homer uses it in subjugating Odysseus to Penelope at the end of the poem. For no one can deny that Penelope is a master of sleep. She goes to bed dozens of times in the course of the story, has lots of sleep shed on her by gods, experiences an array of telling and efficacious dreams and evolves her own theory of how to read them. Moreover, Homer shows us as early as Book 4 that sleep is the deepest contract she shares with her husband. Miles apart, years apart, consciously and unconsciously, they turn the key of each other. So Penelope in Book 4, lying awake in her chamber while the suitors carouse below, is compared by Homer to a lion cornered in a circle of huntsmen. Then she falls asleep, to dream of her husband, "noble Odysseus who has the heart of a lion,"[20] and wake up profoundly soothed. Sleep *works* for Penelope. She knows how to use it, enjoy it, theorize it and even to parody it, should need arise. As in her famous "recognition scene" with Odysseus (which occupies Books 19–23 of the poem).

Penelope's purpose in this scene is to seduce and overcome Odysseus, i.e., to seduce *by* overcoming Odysseus. She goes at it from the sleep side, because there she can win. As we have already seen, and as she probably knows, sleep is not his country. Her seduction has two aspects, first a practical one, the bed question: Who sleeps where? This question culminates in Book 23 in the so-called "trick of the bed," whereby Penelope manoeuvres Odysseus (still disguised as a stranger) into betraying his identity. For she alludes to the bed in her marriage chamber as one that can be moved out into the corridor to accommodate a guest. Odysseus is outraged: as he alone knows, the bed in her chamber was one he carved himself twenty years ago out of an oak tree in the middle of their house. His outrage is the final proof she needs of who he is. But before this recognition quite a bit of sleeping goes on, or is prevented from going on, in noteworthy ways.

Let's look at Book 19, which takes the form of a long conversation between husband and wife before they retire to separate beds, on the night before the climax of the plot. After they have conversed, Penelope instructs her maid-servants to give Odysseus a bath and prepare a luxurious bedstead for him. Odysseus rejects these arrangements, insists on being bathed by an old woman and being given a place on the bare ground to sleep. So Odysseus goes off, has his bath, then returns and sits down beside his wife. Whereupon, instead of saying goodnight, she launches into Penelope's Interpretation of Dreams (to which we'll return in a moment). Finally they do say goodnight and retire— she upstairs to her chamber, he to the ground in the forecourt. So there they are, in separate rooms of the same house, each lying awake. Athene sheds sleep on Penelope at the end of Book 19, then sheds sleep on Odysseus at the begin-ning of Book 20. No sooner does Odysseus fall asleep than Penelope awakes, weeping and crying out. Her voice carries through the house to where Odysseus is sleeping, enters his dream and convinces him that his wife is standing over him in the flesh, recognizing and welcoming him home. Odysseus wakes up, receives an omen from Zeus and rejoices in the forecourt. Homer has woven a strange symbiosis between these two people, together and apart in the same night, entering and exiting each other's minds, almost sharing one consciousness—especially at that moment when Penelope penetrates the membrane of her husband's sleep and fills him with joy. I would call that a successful seduction.

For the theoretical aspect of this seduction, let's return to the long conversation of Book 19. It has two parts. First, husband and wife exchange narratives of what they've been doing for the last twenty years; here Odysseus mainly lies, Penelope tells the truth. Then there is a pause while Odysseus has his bath. Now a bath in epic is often a mechanism of transition to new conditions.[21] After the bath, Penelope takes the conversational initiative and offers a complex (and almost certainly fictitious) narrative about a dream she has had, demanding that Odysseus interpret the dream. Surely this demand is peculiar. The dream is of an eagle who flies down from the sky, slaughters Penelope's twenty pet geese, then announces that he is not an eagle at all, nor a dream, but the real Odysseus returned to save his household. The dream is as blatant as an English movie with English subtitles and Odysseus politely says so. But why does Penelope require his complicity in reading it?

Because it is her game they are playing now: they are reasoning from the sleep side, where she is a master. Look what she does next. Broaches her theory of dreams. Dreams are double, she says, some true, some false. True ones emerge from the gates of horn, false from the gates of ivory. This theory is as bogus as the dream of geese. Penelope is talking through her hat. But all of a sudden, out of her hat, Penelope drops a bombshell. Tomorrow, she announces, I'm going to set up a contest, see which of the suitors can shoot through twelve axes with Odysseus' bow. The winner will take me home as his wife. Here is a sudden practical solution to the whole domestic dilemma. Odysseus hastily agrees it is a great idea. Penelope has orchestrated the conversation so the great idea seems to drop out of a dream—or indeed to shoot out through the very gates of horn. She has involved Odysseus in the interpretive necessity of dreams as he earlier involved her in the autobiographical necessity of lies. She has matched his ambiguities and used her sleep knowledge to wrap him in an act of seduction that he cannot outwit—that he will not wish to outwit. She invites him into the way her mind works. Rather like the moon in the mirror in Elizabeth Bishop's poem "Insomnia":

> The moon in the bureau mirror
> looks out a million miles
> (and perhaps with pride, at herself,
> but she never, never smiles)
> far and away beyond sleep, or
> perhaps she's a daytime sleeper.
>
> By the Universe deserted,
> *she*'d tell it to go to hell,
> and she'd find a body of water,
> or a mirror, on which to dwell.
> So wrap up care in a cobweb
> and drop it down the well
>
> into that world inverted
> where left is always right,
> where the shadows are really the body,
> where we stay awake all night,
> where the heavens are shallow as the sea
> is now deep, and you love me.[22]

As far as love goes, Penelope's only real rival among the female personnel of the *Odyssey* is Nausikaa, the *very* unmarried girl whom Odysseus meets in Book 6 on the island of the Phaiakians. She is asleep when we first meet her:

> ... the girl
> lay sleeping in form and image like to immortals,
> Nausikaa, daughter of great-hearted Alkinoos,
> and alongside her two attendants having beauty from the Graces
> on either side of the pillars. But the brilliant doors were shut.[23]

Homer shows us the sleeper in all her layers of defense. He shows us the doors, pillars, attendants, behind which the she lies. Then he shows us how to pass through doors, in the person of Athene, who traverses the house as a blast of wind and stands over Nausikaa's bed, whispering:

> "*Nausikaa*—how is it your mother bore so slack a girl as you?
> Look, your shining clothes lie in a mess.
> But for you marriage is near, when you will need beautiful things
> to wear yourself and to give to those who attend you.
> ... let's go do laundry as soon as dawn appears."[24]

Athene puts into Nausikaa a word that condenses laundry with marriage (cleanliness with sex), a word whose dream logic names Nausikaa's perfect purity at the very moment we see it most exposed to violation. For there is another motionless presence on this page. Nausikaa lies sleeping side by side with Odysseus, not in the space of her room but in narrative juxtaposition. Two verses describing Odysseus (who is lying naked in a pile of leaves on the outskirts of Nausikaa's city) immediately precede our view of Nausikaa in her bed:

> So there he lay much-enduring goodly Odysseus
> overwhelmed by sleep and exhaustion.[25]

Odysseus' exhaustion subtends and embraces Nausikaa's dream (she rises at v. 50 but he does not wake until 117). Their sleep prefigures everything that will occur between the man and the girl in the days to follow—a system of contradictions curving in and out of impossibility without arriving at refutation, oxymoron of male and female—as the old, wild, dirty, naked, married, shelterless man of many turns coils himself around a girl who lies straight in her nine frames of safety dreaming of laundry.

She is the cleanest girl in epic. And his dirt emphasizes that, not to say the brutal opacity of his sleep—whereas she lies transparent: we watch the dream in her head, we know her action before she does, we see her desire prior to itself. Her desire is to find a pretext and travel far from the city, to where the washing pools lie. But this is precisely where Odysseus lies. The night before, at the end of Book 5, he laid himself down "on the edge of the land" to sleep the sleep of elemental life. Life is all he has left. Wife, child, parents, home, ship, comrades, possessions, clothing, youth, strength and personal fame are all lost. He had to cover himself in a pile of leaves to survive the night:

> And when he saw [the leaf pile]
> much-enduring goodly Odysseus laughed
> and lay in the middle and heaped a big bunch of leaves over himself.
> As when someone hides a firebrand in black embers
> on the edge of the land, who has no other neighbours near,
> preserving the seed of fire, lest he have to kindle a light
> from somewhere else,
> so Odysseus wrapped himself in leaves.[26]

"On the edge of the land" is a symbolic description. "Land" means farmland, cultivated space. "Odysseus is stranded at the margin of culture: he has come back in from the wilderness and preserves within himself (just barely) the means to begin civilization again. But no one can begin civilization alone. And the sleep of fire needs careful waking. Homer seems to enjoy assigning this task to a girl whose chief concerns are cold water and aristocratic hygiene.

Once he is awake, Odysseus finds the island of the Phaiakians a perplexing place. Almost everyone he meets presumes he has come there to marry Nausikaa, inherit her father's kingdom and live happily ever after. It is as if he has waked up inside someone else's dream, only to find himself the protagonist of it. For these dreamlike Phaiakians know who Odysseus is, although he withholds as long as possible from them the news that *he* is Odysseus. And as their local poet performs songs from the epic tradition that tell of Odysseus' exploits at Troy, he sits and weeps to hear himself acclaimed in the third person. He has backed into his own heroic *persona*, like a shadow finding its body.

Or, like Rosencrantz and Guildenstern in Tom Stoppard's play *Rosencrantz and Guildenstern Are Dead*, where two Shakespearean courtiers find themselves in the midst of the tragedy of *Hamlet* without quite understanding who wrote them into the script. Yet they scramble to play their part, manage to produce the right lines and end up dead in England, as Shakespeare's scenario requires. It is not clear whether they are awake or asleep—they talk about having been roused at dawn yet act like people stuck in a bad dream. It is a familiar dream. Stoppard uses the familiarity of Shakespeare's play to lock us into the badness of the bad dream. He puts us, as audience, on the sleep side of the play, alongside Rosencrantz and Guildenstern, while the other characters of *Hamlet* wander in and out muttering passages of Shakespeare's text. Stoppard uses Shakespeare's text to capture Rosencrantz and Guildenstern within his own, in somewhat the same way Virginia Woolf used square brackets to capture the Ramsays and their friends in a long night of sleep. As readers we take a guilty pleasure in these arrangements. For we would almost like to see Rosencrantz and Guildenstern escape their predicament, except it would spoil the plot of *Hamlet*. Good sleepers that we are, we do not quite want to wake up. Stoppard's play praises sleep, functionally, for its necessity. No other experience gives us so primary a sense of being governed by laws outside us. No other substance can so profoundly saturate a story in compulsion, inevitability and dread as sleep can. Mr. Ramsay in square brackets has no option to snatch his wife back from death, nor Rosencrantz and Guildenstern to rewrite the tragedy of *Hamlet*. It is, as Virginia Woolf says, useless to ask the night these questions. Stoppard allows his character Guildenstern to ask them anyway. Guildenstern is a kind of amateur philosopher; he derives consolation in the middle of the play from a well-known Taoist parable about waking and sleeping:

> Guildenstern: Wheels have been set in motion, and they have their own pace, to which we are . . . condemned. Each move is dictated by the previous one—that is the meaning of order. If we start being arbitrary it'll just be a shambles: at least let us hope so. Because if we happened, just happened to discover, or even suspect, that our spontaneity is part of their order, we'd know we were lost. *(He sits.)* A Chinaman of the T'ang dynasty—and by which definition a philosopher—dreamed he was a butterfly, and from that moment he was never quite sure that he was not a butterfly dreaming it was a Chinese philosopher. Envy him; in his two-fold security.[27]

There is something cheesy about Guildenstern's envy, about his use of the parable of the butterfly and the sage (traditionally ascribed to Zhuang Zi, who was not of the T'ang dynasty), about his philosophizing in general, that makes me happy to turn to a different amateur philosopher for my final example of the praise of sleep. Sokrates, arguably the most amateur and the most different of the philosophers of the Western tradition, exhibits, in the Platonic dialogues describing the final days of his life, a certain regard for that sublime residue, the tear of sleep.

Let's consider the *Krito*. Plato begins this dialogue in the dark, with Sokrates starting up sheer from sleep and his dream still wet on its back. Here are the opening lines of the dialogue:

Sokrates:	Why are you here? Isn't it early?
Krito:	Yes pretty early.
Sokrates:	What time?
Krito:	Near dawn.
Sokrates:	I'm surprised the guard let you in.
Krito:	Oh he knows me by now. Anyway I tip him.
Sokrates:	So did you just arrive or have you been here awhile?
Krito:	Quite awhile.
Sokrates:	Why didn't you wake me?[28]

And so it emerges that Krito sat watching Sokrates sleep because he looked happy sleeping and Krito had nothing to wake him for but his death day. Perhaps I should call to mind the situation here. The *Krito* is the third of a tetralogy of dialogues concerned with Sokrates' trial, imprisonment and death. Sokrates has by now been judged guilty and is in jail awaiting execution. His death is postponed because his trial coincided with the annual Athenian mission to Delos, during which no prisoners could be executed. Krito has come to announce to Sokrates that the ship from Delos has been sighted and so his death will take place the next day. To which news Sokrates responds:

Sokrates:	You know I don't think so. It won't be tomorrow.
Krito:	What are you talking about?
Sokrates:	I had a dream last night—lucky you didn't wake me!
Krito:	What dream?
Sokrates:	A beautiful woman came up to me, dressed in white, called to me and said: *Sokrates, on the third day you shall reach rich Phthia.*
Krito:	Weird dream, Sokrates.
Sokrates:	Well it seems obvious to me.[29]

Plato has constructed the opening of this dialogue in such a way as to align the realms of waking and sleeping, drawing our attention to an active boundary between them—active because it leaks. Sokrates brings a bit of difference back with him from the sleep side. The words of the woman in white contain a hint of the argument that will carry Sokrates all the way from these sleepy sentences to his death at the end of the *Phaedo*. She tells Sokrates he will reach Phthia on the third day. It is a line from Homer. In the ninth book of the *Iliad* Achilles receives an embassy of Greeks sent by Agamemnon to persuade him to return to war, promising tons of gifts if he does. He responds with a 114-line denunciation of gifts, war and Agamemnon, including a threat to leave for home at once:

"On the third day I could reach rich Phthia."[30]

Phthia is Achilles' homeland. It is also a name cognate with a Greek verb for death (*phthiein*) but that may be incidental. Let us observe some analogies between these two heroes heading for Phthia on the third day: both Sokrates and Achilles are eccentric gentlemen who find themselves defying the rules of life of their society and disappointing the hopes of a circle of intense friends. For, as Achilles is surrounded by Achaians urging him to resume life as a warrior, Sokrates is surrounded by Athenians urging him to escape prison and take up life in exile. Both of them say *no* to their friends. Both argue this choice on the basis of an idiosyncratic understanding of the word *psyche*, "soul, spirit, principle of life." So Achilles repudiates Agamemnon's offer of gifts in these terms:

"All the gifts and treasure in Troy aren't worth as much as my own soul!"[31]

And Sokrates explains his choice for death at the end of the *Phaedo* by saying,

"Since the soul seems to be immortal . . . a man [who has lived a good life] might as well be cheerful as he makes his exit into Hades."[32]

Who knows what either of them means by *psyche* or whether "soul" is a reasonable translation of it. Still we can say they both use this word to indicate some kind of immortal value, some sort of transcendent attractor, that exerts such a strong pressure on their mortal lives and thinking as to pull them into a choice that strikes everyone around them as insane. I reckon that Plato in his dialogues involving Sokrates had somewhat the same literary problem as Homer in his *Iliad*, viz., to convey a hero in his *difference* from other people, a hero whose power over other people arose in part from something *incognito* in his very being. In the dialogues that record his last days, the Platonic Sokrates seems increasingly a person ungraspable in ordinary sentences, a person who is (to use a current expression) *coming from somewhere else.*

Plato shows him coming from the sleep side in the *Krito*. As if he had slept in the temple of Asklepios, Sokrates emerges from his dream "seeing with both eyes." And he does not hesitate to trust what the woman in white has let him see, although Krito dismisses it. The woman in white will turn out to be correct. Sokrates is inclined to trust, and to be correct about trusting, different sources of knowledge than other philosophers do—like his crazy *daimon*, or the oracle of Apollo, not to say the good sentences of sleep. Sokrates also puts a fair amount of faith in his own poetic imagination—his power to turn nothing into something. So in the latter half of the *Krito*, since Krito can think of nothing further to say, Sokrates conducts both sides of an imaginary conversation between himself as Sokrates and a ventriloquized projection of the *Nomoi*, the Laws of Athens. These ventriloquized Laws are as weird as the ghosts that Virginia Woolf sent rustling and whispering around the rooms of her "Haunted House," looking for their buried treasure. If you recall, that story of the haunted house ends with a spooky moment of dispossession, as the ghosts lean over the sleeper's bed and discover *their* treasure buried in *her* heart. Sokrates also suffers a moment of dispossession at the end of the *Krito*. The voices of the Laws, he says, fill his prison cell and drown out all other sound. He has to stop talking:

> "O beloved friend Krito, these voices are what I seem to hear—as Korybantic worshippers imagine they hear flutes—and the sound of their words is so loud in me, I am deaf to everything else."[33]

So Sokrates falls silent, overcome by what Virginia Woolf might call "the singing of the real world."

To sum up.
I shall state my conclusions in the form of an "Ode to Sleep."

ODE TO SLEEP

Think of your life without it.
Without that slab of outlaw time punctuating every pillow—without pillows.
Without the big black kitchen and the boiling stove where you
snatch morsels
of your own father's legs and arms
only to see them form into a sentence
which—*you weep with sudden joy*—will save you
if you can remember it
later! Later,
not much left but a pale green *upsilon* embalmed between *butter* and *fly*—
but what's that stuff he's dabbing in your eye?
It is the moment when the shiver stops.
A shiver is a perfect servant.
Her amen sootheth.
"As a matter of fact," she confides in a footnote, "it was
a misprint for *mammoth.*"
It hurts me to know this.
Exit wound, as they say.

1. In his essay *On Prophecy in Sleep,* Aristotle reads sleep as part of nature and dreams as messages from the realm of the daimonic, which lies between divine and human being (463b12–15): Aristotle, *Parva Naturalia,* ed. W. D. Ross (Oxford: Clarendon Press, 1955). Translations are my own unless otherwise noted.

2. Immanuel Kant, *Anthropology from a Pragmatic View,* trans. M. J. Gregor (The Hague: Martinus Nijhoff, 1974), 85.

3. John Keats, *Complete Poems,* ed. J. Stillinger (Cambridge, Mass.: The Belknap Press of Harvard Univ. Press, 1978, 1982).

4. Elizabeth Bishop, *The Complete Poems: 1927–1979* (New York: Farrar, Straus and Giroux, 1979, 1983), 14.

5. *Inscriptiones Graecae:* vol. IV, *Inscriptiones Argolidis,* ed. M. Fraenkel (Berlin: Berlin Academy, 1902), 223–24.

6. Virginia Woolf, *To the Lighthouse* (New York: Harcourt, Brace, 1927), 128; 133; 134.

7. Ibid., 193.

8. Virginia Woolf, *The Diary of Virginia Woolf,* eds. A. O. Bell and A. McNeillie (London: The Hogarth Press, 1980), 3.260: Oct. 11, 1929.

9. Virginia Woolf, *The Waves* (New York: Harcourt Brace Jovanovich, 1931), 292.

10. Virginia Woolf, *The Voyage Out* (London: Duckworth, 1915), 59.

11. Virginia Woolf, *A Haunted House and Other Stories* (London: The Hogarth Press, 1944), 11.

12. Homer, *Iliad,* eds. W. Leaf and M. A. Bayfield (London, 1895), 23.103.

13. Virginia Woolf, *To the Lighthouse,* 128.

14. Homer, *Odyssey,* ed. W. B. Stanford (London: Macmillan, 1947) 1.433–34.

15. Ibid., 15.7–8.

16. Ibid., 1.215–16.

17. Ibid., 19.50.

18. Ibid., 10.47–52.

19. Ibid., 12.371–72.

20. Ibid., 4.514.

21. This scene, where Odysseus is recognized by his old nurse Eurykleia because of the scar on his leg, is analyzed by Eric Auerbach in *Mimesis,* trans. W. Trask (Garden City: Doubleday, 1957); Penelope seems unaware.

22. Elizabeth Bishop, *The Complete Poems,* 70.

23. Homer, *Odyssey,* 6.15–19.

24. Ibid., 6.25–30.

25. Ibid., 6.1–2.

26. Ibid., 5.486–91.

27. Tom Stoppard, *Rosencrantz and Guildenstern Are Dead* (London: Faber and Faber, 1967) 51.

28. Plato, *Krito,* 43a–b, in *Platonis Opera,* ed. J. Burnet (Oxford: Clarendon Press, 1976), vol. 1.

29. Ibid., 43d–44b.

30. Homer, *Iliad,* 9.363.

31. Ibid., 9.401.

32. Plato, *Phaedo,* 114d–115a, in *Platonis Opera,* vol. 1.

33. Plato, *Krito,* 54d.

FOAM

(Essay with Rhapsody)

On the Sublime in Longinus and Antonioni

The Sublime is a documentary technique. "Documentary: of, related to or relying on documentation; objective, factual" *(Oxford English Dictionary)*. Take Longinus' treatise *On the Sublime*. This work is an aggregation of quotes. It has muddled arguments, little organization, no paraphrasable conclusion. Its attempts at definition are incoherent or tautological. Its key topic (passion) is deferred to another treatise (which does not exist). You will come away from reading its (unfinished) forty chapters with no clear idea what the Sublime actually is. But you will have been thrilled by its documentation. Longinus skates from Homer to Demosthenes to Moses to Sappho on blades of pure bravado. What is a quote? A quote (cognate with *quota*) is a cut, a section, a slice of someone else's orange. You suck the slice, toss the rind, skate away. Part of what you enjoy in a documentary technique is the sense of banditry. To loot someone else's life or sentences and make off with a point of view, which is called "objective" because you can make anything into an object by treating it this way, is exciting and dangerous. Let us see who controls the danger.

In Chapter 20 of *On the Sublime*, Longinus congratulates the Greek orator Demosthenes because he knows how to make his nouns rain like blows when recounting a violent scene:

> By attitude! by look! by voice! the man who hits can do things to the other which the other can't even describe.[1]

"With words like these"—Longinus smiles—"the orator produces the same effect as the man who hits—striking the judges' minds with blow after blow"—and he quotes again:

By attitude! look! voice! when he with insolence, when he like an enemy, when he with bare fists, when he with a slap on the side of your head—[2]

Longinus' point is that, by brutal juxtaposition of coordinate nouns or noun clauses, Demosthenes transposes violence of fists into violence of syntax. His facts spill over the frame of their original context and pummel the judges' minds. Watch this spillage, which moves from the man who hits, to the words of Demosthenes describing him, to the judges hearing these words, to Longinus analyzing the whole process, to me recalling Longinus' discussion of it and finally to you reading my account. The passionate moment echoes from soul to soul. Each controls it temporarily. Each enjoys it quote by quote.

Why does a soul enjoy it? Longinus answers this question by addressing the psychology of watching, listening, reading, being an audience. This psychology involves a shift and opening out of power:

> Touched by the true sublime your soul is naturally lifted up, she rises to a proud height, is filled with joy and vaunting, as if she had herself created this thing that she has heard.[3]

To feel the joy of the Sublime is to be inside creative power for a moment, to share a bit of electric extra life with the artist's invention, to spill with him. Consider another example. When Michaelangelo Antonioni was filming *Story of a Love Affair* with actress Lucia Bosé in 1950, he found he had to step out from behind the camera, cross the set and adjust her psychology himself:

> How many blows Lucia took for the final scene! The film ended with her beaten and sobbing, in a doorway. But she was always happy and it was hard for her to pretend to be desperate. She was not an actress. To obtain

the results I wanted I had to use insults, abuse, hard slaps. In the end she broke down and wept like a child. She played her part wonderfully.[4]

Inbetween Antonioni and Lucia in the doorway is an area of danger. It is a documentary danger. I mean this in two ways. "Documentary" implies, cinematically, a preference for factual over fictional subject matter in the preparation of a film. When he steps from behind the camera and crosses down into *Story* to improve Lucia Bosé with his wonderful slaps, Antonioni plunders a boundary between her and her part. "Documentary" also refers to a dependence on documents. Who would know of this incident had Antonioni not told it to a reporter from *Corriere della Sera* in 1978 and reprinted it in his book *The Architecture of Vision*—acting as his own Demosthenes and then as his own Longinus? So too we might never have known of Demosthenes' effect on a courtroom of judges had Longinus not praised it in *On the Sublime*. We might never have known of the violence of "the man who hits" had Demosthenes not denounced it in his speech *Against Meidias*. In each case a passionate moment is created, quoted, spilled. You may feel your own hands tingle, your soul lift.

The original expert in this kind of spilling of power, Longinus tells us, was Homer. Here is Longinus describing how Homer crosses down into his own poem to become as sublime as his subject matter:

> Look this is the real Homer who storms like a wind alongside the fighting men, none other than Homer who "rages as when spearshaking Ares or ruinous fire in the mountains rages, in folds of deep forest, and foam is around his mouth."[5]

Foam is the sign of an artist who has sunk his hands into his own story, and also of a critic storming and raging in folds of his own deep theory. It is apparent to most of his readers that Longinus moves through the chapters of *On the Sublime* covered with foam himself. "Longinus *is* the great Sublime he draws," says Boileau. "What is most Sublime, Homer's battle of the gods or Longinus' apostrophe upon it?" asks Gibbon. "Sublime natures are seldom clean!" is Longinus' way of putting it.[6] Slap.

S T O P

The Sublime is big. "Bigness," or "magnitude," is one of Longinus' synonyms for it throughout his treatise. Its bigness is always threatening to go out of control, to submerge and vanquish the soul that seeks to enjoy it. Threat provides the Sublime with its essential structure, an alternation of danger and salvation, which other aesthetic experiences (e.g., beauty) do not seem to share. Threat also furnishes the Sublime with its necessary content—dire things (volcanoes, oceans, ecstasies) and dire reactions (death, dread, transport) within which the sublime soul is *all but lost.*

Foam is a sign of how close the threat came. In fact a sublime soul is threatened not only from without but from within, for this soul's own nature is too big for itself. The sublime orator, the sublime poet, the sublime critic, is a man wildly lost in his own art, hurried out of himself, heedless, rash, wrong—"they burn all before them as they are carried along!"[7] Longinus insists on ecstasy, on genius spinning out of control, like the Rhine or the Danube or even Mount Aetna, "whose uprushings send rocks and whole riverbanks from down below and pour out rivers of that weird, spontaneous, earthborn fire."[8] At the same time he likes to pause on the brink of Aetna, observe its monstrous spillage, toy with conceptual control:

> "Could we not say of all such examples that . . . the monstrous always excites wonder!"[9]

Antonioni's films involve different kinds of playing with the passionate moment, different ways of spilling its contents. He enjoys, for example, drawing attention to offscreen space by placing a mirror in the middle of the scene so that you glimpse a stray piece of world there. Or he likes to give you two successive shots of the same portion of reality, first from close up, then a little further away, scarcely different yet noticeably not the same. He also uses a procedure, called *temps mort* by French critics, whereby the camera is left running on a scene after the actors think they have finished acting it:

> When everything has been said, when the scene appears to be finished, there is what comes afterward. . . . the actors continue out of inertia into moments that seem "dead." The actor commits "errors." . . .[10]

Antonioni likes to document these moments of error, when the actors do unscheduled things, act "back to front" as he says. Possibility of foam. He began opening out the frame in this way while working on *Story of a Love Affair*. Later he took to letting the shot run even after the actors had made their exit. As if for a while something might be still rustling around there in an empty doorway.

Whether or not Antonioni's films are sublime, Antonioni's use of Antonioni is sublime. As is Longinus' use of Longinus. "Sublimity is the echo of a great mind—as I believe I have written somewhere else" (9.2), says Longinus, echoing gently.[11] You get an echo effect from Antonioni too, especially when he tells the story about the day he went to the asylum, which is repeated in every interview, conversation or study of his work. He says the first time he put his eye to the camera was in a lunatic asylum.[12] He had determined to make a film on the insane. The director of the asylum looked insane too, or so Antonioni noted when he met him on the day of the shoot. But the inmates themselves were efficient and helpful in setting up props and equipment and getting the room ready.

"I must say I was surprised by their good cheer," he says. And then he turned on his big lights.

The room "became hell." Inmates were screaming. They crumpled, twisted and rolled themselves over the floor, trying to get away. Antonioni stood numb, his cameraman too. At last the director of the asylum yelled, "Off with the lights!" The room grew silent with a slow and feeble movement of bodies leaving agony behind. Antonioni says he never forgot this scene. Had he shot film that day, it would have been a documentary of foam. But the mad people, who understood spillage, did not wish to be quoted. You have to admire the mad. They know how to value a passionate moment. So does Longinus. His treatise ends like this:

> Best to leave these matters and to proceed to what comes next—the passions, concerning which I undertook to write in another. . . .

—here the manuscript of *On the Sublime* breaks off. The next page is too damaged to read and after that you cannot say how much is missing. Longinus skates away.

THE DAY ANTONIONI CAME TO THE ASYLUM
(Rhapsody)

It was a restless moment. He came closer.
—Lucia Bosé

It was the sound of her writing that woke me. Since you ask, this is what I remember. Her desk is just outside my room. Some days I hear sounds too loud. Some days I hear a crowd and there is no crowd.

At her desk she keeps notes. She lists our medications. She does the crossword puzzle or puts checkmarks in the margins of *Classified*. A little dry grinding sound. Others are unaware. These differences are hard to bear.

Then there it was, mutiny. They told us we had to come downstairs to the salon early and "participate," so we all took our clothes off. Eighteen naked people in the hall. She said not a word. That's what scared us. We got dressed again. Overalls, no more women and men.

What the eye saw was a pile of documents on her desk with tiny paragraphs and signatures and staples. These documents were not seen again in the salon or elsewhere. I keep my eye on documents. Documents are how most of us ended up here. *That's him,* said someone as we descended the stairs. Antonioni wore a small brown sweater and looked like a cat. I wanted to give him a lick or a pat.

Swoony was the mood I would say in the room. A suddenly arriving beautiful man will not so much fool people as keep them awake—drunk with our own awakeness we rushed around doing his bidding. To be awake was a thing many had dreamed of, while continuing to sleep for years, like the famous princess in her coffin of glass. Once I opened a Chinese fortune cookie that said, *Some will attain their heart's desire, alas.*

He got behind his 16mm Bell & Howell. Two of his men gave instructions. Patty and Bates and I were dragging chairs out of the way. The big black cords had to be run out to plugs. We were making no mistakes. We were being extremely careful. No jokes. No sleep. No staring. And she in her place by the wall, refolding her crossword and trying to look calm. Because it contains the word "hyssop" the 51st is my favourite Psalm.

Hyssop is (as you may know) a purificatory herb that smells like mint from outer space. *Create in me a clean heart, O God.* I got a whiff of hyssop just when those big black cords lit (light starts to smell when there's too much of it) and some sudden radiance aligned me with the rugs on the floor. So there we all were on the floor and Patty yelled *Keep turning* so we did (to ward off death) and every time Bates turned past me we kissed which is one of our interior arrangements in group activities (of which there are a lot here), life being short and burning yearning being burning yearning.

Patty's view is that if I weren't in this place I wouldn't have time for someone like Bates. I told her I'm a practical fellow and Bates is my practice right now. "Have time for" is exactly the point—

days here are two hundred years long. Outsiders (Antonioni) come in at the wrong velocity. I bet he knew that. His face had the look of someone who enters a room and there is no floor. Meanwhile we rolled all the way to the wall and at a signal from Patty reversed and rolled back—beautifully, I thought, it was somehow like bowling. Antonioni seemed pained by everyone yowling.

To yell is the rule here—rule of the mad—it disguises the kissing and makes us less sad.

Antonioni opened his eyes. She left her place by the wall and came over to him. *The patients are afraid of the light,* she explained, *they think it is a monster.* This kind of spontaneous misinformation is typical of the medical profession. Well I suppose she could hardly say, *The patients worship life-giving Aphrodite every chance they get, thank you for furnishing this opportunity.* Anyway I'm not sure how smart she is. One day I told her about evolution—how in the beginning people didn't have selves as we have selves, there were arms heads torsos what have you roaming about by the breakers of the shore of life, ankles unattached, eyes needing brows, until at last what made the parts come together as whole creatures was Love—and she said, *Do you know a six-letter word for loose or wanton woman derived from the sound of a horse's hooves going down the road at night?* To which I replied, *Yes I do and I can shower with Bates tonight, right?*

Always planning ahead that's me, practical as purgatory my mom used to say. *That the bones which thou hast broken may rejoice.* But now there we were eighteen terrible people in a room trying not to look at one another as we got up off the floor. Antonioni gave himself a tidy cat shake and returned to form. The director of the asylum was beside him murmuring low in a Let's See What We've Learned Today tone. Sober nods all round. I would have liked to hear from Antonioni. Cats don't spend themselves but they notice everything. I saw he noticed Bates. How close for an instant we grazed our fates.

New white snow had fallen over dark slush outside. Patty expressed disappointment in the morning's pitch and tenor overall. *Fuckin sketchy gig, man*—was I believe her phrasing. Still we take our blessings where they fall. Nothing improves community life like an hour of aerobics first thing. The yelling is mild all the rest of the day. *Purge me and I shall be clean, wash me and I shall be whiter than snow.* And it was Friday, angel cake for supper, hot showers later and who knows what interior arrangements there. Since the day I gave her "tittup" she treats me with extra care. *Don't be a mourner,* she says and juts way back on two legs of her chair.

NOTES

1. Longinus, *On the Sublime,* ed. W. Rhys Roberts (Cambridge: Cambridge University Press, 1907), 20.2; Demosthenes, *Against Meidias* (Oration 21), ed. D. M. MacDowell (Oxford: Clarendon, 1990), 72.

2. Longinus, *On the Sublime,* 20.2.

3. Ibid., 7.2.

4. Michaelangelo Antonioni, *The Architecture of Vision* (New York: 1996), 40.

5. Longinus, *On the Sublime,* 9.11; Homer, *Iliad,* ed. W. Leaf and M. A. Bayfield (London: Macmillan & Co., 1895), 15.605–7.

6. Longinus, *On the Sublime,* 33.1.

7. Ibid., 33.2.

8. Ibid., 35.4.

9. Ibid., 35.5.

10. Seymour Chatwin, *Antonioni, or, the Surface of the World* (Berkeley: Univ. of California Press, 1985), 126 and 24n.

11. Longinus, *On the Sublime,* 9.2.

12. Originally in "Fare un film è per me vivere," in *Cinema nuovo* 138 (1959).

SUBLIMES

Everything might spill.

LONGINUS' DREAM OF ANTONIONI

Long bright dream of waking beside a man bleeding from the eyes. Clots of blood on his face and through the bedclothes and him not inclined to take it seriously. In the kitchen later one of his gambling pals surmised he had been poisoned by an enemy at the casino using a powder which, mixed into a drink, slowly ruins the eyes from inside. I sent him to consult a doctor while I made breakfast in the kitchen already vaguely crowded with his friends. He returned saying the doctor gave him only winks and ribald jokes about "going courting." Sad now I turned my attention to the coffee pot with its missing parts and melted cord.

Searching for things sublime I walked up into the muddy windy big hills
behind the town where trees riot according to their own laws and

one may

observe so many methods of moving green—under, over, around, across,
up the back, higher, fanning, condensing, rifled, flat in the eyes, as if

pacing a

cell, like a litter of grand objects, minutely, absorbed, one leaf at a time,
ocean-furious, nettle-streaked, roping along, unmowed, fresh out of pools,

clear as Babel,

such a tower! scattered through the heart, green in the strong sense, dart-shook,
crownly, carrying the secrets of its own heightening on

up, juster than a shot, gloomier than Milton or even his king of terrors, idol in
its dark parts, as a word coined to mean "storm (of love)" or

"waving lines"

(architectural), scorned, clean, with blazing nostrils, not a
servant, not rapid, rapid.

L'
(Ode to Monica Vitti)

l' (never
anywhere
simply absent
or—how
plunged does the mind have to be)
Avventura : caught
in the time of the island, scraping themselves back and forth over
the rocks, men slant against the wind and her golden
hair going horizontal in whips on the ecstatic sea, boats roar
up, roar off, men stand
gazing—
and as
for the scandal of our abandonment
in a universe of "sudden trembling love," blondes
being
always
fatally
reinscribed
on an old cloth
faintly,
interminably
undone, why
does Plato

call Necessity
a "wandering cause" isn't it because
you can
't
tell
where
she got in?—men steady on the rock
now they have put that gilded night
down
a little rip in their minds.

ODE TO THE SUBLIME BY MONICA VITTI

I want everything.
Everything is a naked thought that strikes.

A foghorn sounding through fog makes the fog seem to be everything.
Quail eggs eaten from the hand in fog make everything aphrodisiac.

My husband shrugs when I say so, my husband shrugs at everything.
The lakes where his factory has poisoned everything are as beautiful as Brueghel.

I keep my shop, in order that I may sell everything there, empty but I
leave the light on.
Everything might spill.

Do you know that in the deepest part of the sea everything goes transparent?
asks my husband's friend Corrado and I say Do you know how afraid I am?

Everything requires attention, I never relax my neck even when kissing Corrado.
"Everything," Kant says, exists only in our mind, attended by
a motion of pleasure and

pain that throws itself back and forth in me when I lay on Corrado's
bed fighting with everything with Corrado watching from across
the room then he came to the bed and

mounted me and this made no difference except now I had to fight everything
through Corrado, which I did
"undaunted" (so Kant) on his freezing bed in its midnight glare.

What will you take? I ask Corrado who is leaving for Patagonia and when
he says 2 or 3
valises I say If I had to go away I would take with me *everything I see.*

To this Corrado says nothing which is not I think the opposite of everything.
Doesn't seem right is what my husband would say, he says
this about everything—

especially since I came out of the clinic, a clinic for people who want everything,
everything I see everything I taste everything I touch
everyday even the ashtrays and at

the clinic I had only one question *What shall I do with my eyes?*

MIA MOGLIE (LONGINUS' RED DESERT)

A caught woman is something the movies want to believe in.
  "For instance, Sappho," as Longinus says.

   greener

Caught from within, she has somehow got the Sublime inside her.
  "As though these could combine and form one body."

    than

Her body vibrates, she is always cold, there is a certain
  cold industrial noise, she is also hot, has stuck a thermometer

    grass

under her arm and forgotten it and at the wall she turns glistening,
  aghast: your prey. "Are you not amazed?"

     and

In sex she clusters herself on the man's body as if hit by a wind.
  "For she is terrified."

       dead

67

On the street she pulls herself along, *to get there will be worse.*
   "For she is all but dying."

almost

The husband speaks of her *time in the clinic,* her *accident.*
   "Not one passion in her but a synod of passions."

I

In the clinic she met a girl whose problem was *she wanted everything.*
   Bolts of everything hit the table.

seem

Now she is well she says of this girl who has turned out to be herself.
   "Sublimity is the echo of a great soul."

to me

What is that antenna for? she asks a man. *To listen to the noise
   of stars—* "as I believe I said," Longinus adds.

68

Comparative figures: 1784 Kant owned 550 books, Goethe 2300, Herder 7700.

Windows: Kant had one bedroom window, which he kept shut at all times, to forestall insects. The windows of his study faced the garden, on the other side of which was the city jail. In summer loud choral singing of the inmates wafted in. Kant asked that the singing be done *sotto voce* and with windows closed. Kant had friends at city hall and got his wish.

Tolstoy: Tolstoy thought that if Kant had not smoked so much tobacco *The Critique of Pure Reason* would have been written in language you could understand (in fact he smoked one pipe at 5 AM).

Numbering: Kant never ate dinner alone, it exhausts the spirit. Dinner guests, in the opinion of the day, should not number more than the Muses nor less than the Graces. Kant set six places.

Sensualism: Kant's favourite dinner was codfish.

Rule Your Nature: Kant breathed only through his nose.

It was hidden in her and it gave Kant pleasure.
L' Eclisse *begins with a wind blowing Monica Vitti's hair. She is inside a room.*

Kant's was a partly negative pleasure.
Where is that wind from?

Kant took pleasure in what he called Thing in Itself.
She is prowling the room with her eyes down, observed deeply
by a man in an armchair.

Thing in Itself was unattainable, insurmountable.
She keeps trying to leave the room.

Nor could Thing in Itself be represented.
Curtains are drawn, the room is full of objects, lamps are burning here and there,
who knows what hour of the night it may be? Her hair blows slowly.

Yet through the very failure of its representation, Thing in Itself might be
inscribed within phenomena.
She lifts a piece of paper, puts it down.

Kant noted a rustling aside of sensible barriers.
Her unquiet drifts in her, spills, drifts on.

A rotating fan is shown sitting on the table beside the man in the armchair.
Kant felt weak as a wave.

Now she can leave. The surface of the movie relaxes.
Kant let his soul expand.

She walks out into the filthy daylight.
Kant pulled his hat down firmly.

She is a little ashamed but glad to be walking.
Off into this more difficult dawn.

71

STANZAS, SEXES, SEDUCTIONS

It's good to be neuter.
     I want to have meaningless legs.
          There are things unbearable.
               One can evade them a long time.
Then you die.

The oceans remind me
     of your green room.
          There are things unbearable.
               Scorn, princes, this little size
of dying.

My personal poetry is a failure.
     I do not want to be a person.
          I want to be unbearable.
               Lover to lover, the greenness of love.
Cool, cooling.

Earth bears no such plant.
     Who does not end up
          a female impersonator?
               Drink all the sex there is.
Still die.

I tempt you.
     I blush.
          There are things unbearable.
          Legs alas.
Legs die.

Rocking themselves down,
     crazy slow,
          some ballet term for it—
               fragment of foil, little
spin,
     little drunk,
          little do,
               little oh,
                    alas.

SPRING BREAK
Swallow Song

One April we drove all the way from Canada to Carolina my father mother
brother and I.

swallow song

Stayed in a motel sand in the sheets sand in the car sand in our pockets months
after we got home.

swallow song is a begging song

Ocean air plush as kissing or the secret parts of plants secrets were dropping out
of us there.

swallow song is a begging song
open up

Walking through a restaurant all together to our table past eyes and sugarbowls
we realized—

swallow song is a begging song
open up
or I'll cry off the door

same moment he did—my brother's shame of us. We saw girls notice him, stiffening their backs.

> *swallow song is a begging song*
> > *open up*
> > > *or I'll cry off the lintel,*
> > > > *the door, the wife within*
> > > *open up*

Loneliness hit. It bleached our lips. I like the word *caesura* but I didn't know it then.

> *swallow song is a begging song*

We knew tans. Fates. Finery! Finery among us. We drove home. Parked in our quiet driveway

> *easily will I cry her off*

(the forsythia had bloomed). Went into the kitchen. Stood with our bags. Hum of the clock on the stove.

> *swallow has come, has come, has come*
> > *who begs the beautiful hours*

My mother put down two crates of oranges beside the fridge. Straightened up,
hand on her back.

> *who begs the turnings of the years*

> > *open up or I*
> *open up or I*
> *open up or I*

Fish sticks for supper? she said to no one in particular.

GUILLERMO'S SIGH SYMPHONY

Do you hear sighing.
    Do you wake amid a sigh.
        Radio sighs AM,
        FM.
            Shortwave sighs crackle in from the Atlantic.
        Hot sighs steam in the dawn.
    People kissing stop to sigh then kiss again.
Doctors sigh into wounds and the bloodstream is changed forever.
      Flowers sigh and two noon bees float backwards.
        Is it doubt.
          Is it disappointment.
            The world didn't owe me anything.
              Leaves come sighing in the door.
         Bits of girl sigh like men.
      Forgeries sigh twice.
Balthus sighs and lies about it, claiming it was Byron's sigh.
      A sigh may come too late.
        Is it better than screaming.
           Give me all your sighs for four or five dollars.

A sigh is weightless,
yet it may interrupt the broadcast.
Can you abstain.
What is that hush that carries itself up each sigh.
We hunt together the sigh and I,
sport of kings.
To want to stop is beyond us.
The more sighs shine the more I'm in trouble—some kind of silvery stuff—
you thought it was the sea?

BLENDED TEXT

You have captured: *pinned* upon
my heart: the wall of *my heart* is your love
with one glance: as *one*
with one bead: as *an exile of the kings* of royalty
of your eyes: *my heart*
you have something of mine: a torn thing
again the moon: *now*
the rule: (who knows)

SWIMMING IN CIRCLES IN COPENHAGEN

The palace guards, the palace guards
      telephoned to ask for shards.
            I sent out the hard dogs.

         Dark swallow.

It is no simple red, he said.
      Each thread
            spun from a different reason for marrying.

         Dark swallow.

This sparkle of anyone, all too soon.
      All too,
            all too soon flaming.

         Dark swallow.

Claiming to have no word for "desire,"
      you brimming burning *glukupikros* liar,
      you candybitter being.

         Dark swallow.

I defy you to find those deep approaches
      where ordinary air is.
            The tough wound plucks itself.

        Dark swallow.

Between grief and nothing
      I'd take grief (Jean Seberg)
            I'd take nothing (Jean-Paul Belmondo).
Perhaps we overvalue conversation.

        Dark swallow.

The palace thief, the palace thief
      overturned his dear ones leaf by leaf.
           For his eyes loved faint things.

        Dark swallow you.

The palace vices, the palace vices
      are obvious as salt prices.
           Poor blue boys went looking for a stark market.

Dark swallow you do.

Only the human can fall out of being (philosophers say)
      or dread this all day.
            I got out, closed the car door, they looked straight ahead.

Dark swallow you do.

On the palace (stone blood paper) ash, the palace ash
      I wrote your name and asked for cash.
            Funny, no one grins in pornography.

Dark swallow you do return.

If I dip myself in this acid are you sure
      my devils will bleach away to pure?
            Giggling and beautiful they stood in the doorway
                discussing their erections.

Dark swallow you do return.

Jean Seberg drove off looking for candy.
I wrote "salt."
Funny.

Dark swallow you do return.
Dark swallow you do return.
Dark swallow you do return
but not to my balcony.

With deep love,
your Master.

GNOSTICISMS

GNOSTICISM I

Heaven's lips! I dreamed
of a page in a book containing the word *bird* and I
entered *bird*.
Bird grinds on,

grinds on, thrusting against black. Thrusting
wings, thrusting again, hard
banks slap against it either side, that bird was exhausted.

Still, beating, working its way and below in dark woods
small creatures
leap. Rip

at food with scrawny lips.
Lips at night.
Nothing guiding it, bird beats on, night wetness on it.
A lion looks up.
Smell of adolescence in these creatures, this ordinary
night for them. Astonishment

inside me like a separate person,
sweat-soaked. How to grip.
For some people a bird sings, feathers shine. I just get this *this*.

GNOSTICISM II

Forgot? how the mind goes at it, you open
the window (late) there is a siffling sound,
that cold smell before sleep, roofs,
frozen staircase, frozen stair,
a piece of it comes in.

Comes in, stands in the room a bit of a column of it alive.
At first no difference then palely, a dust,
an indentation, stain
of some guest
centuries ago.

Some guest *at this very hour,* was it final love or the usual
I said! you said! oh the body,
no listen, unpinning itself, slam of car door,
snow. Far, far, far, far.

Washed in the blood of that.

GNOSTICISM III

First line has to make your brain race that's how Homer does it,
that's how Frank O'Hara does it, why
at such a pace
Muses
slam through the house—there goes one (fainting) up the rungs
of your strange BULLFIGHT, buttered
almost in a nearness
to skyblue
Thy pang—Pollock yourself!
Just to hang on to life is why

GNOSTICISM IV

They found the dog! Mother died! He didn't mean to hang up just
a bad connection! No time for lipstick if I answer that but isn't
there a Ladies outside Philosophy anyway they never start
till ten after oh rats now I've lost the Gertrude Stein
quote was it beefsteak?—what

swarm of clearnesses and do they amaze you,
inbetween when you hear the phone and when you get it,
all palpable explanations of why it rang and what to do
and what'd it be like if your brain were this fit
all the time? Say,

at the moment in the interminable dinner when Coetzee basking
icily across from you at the faculty table is all at once
there like a fox in a glare, asking
And what are your interests?
his face a glass that has shattered but not yet fallen.

GNOSTICISM V

". . . what the little word *after* means . . ."
—I. Kant, *Inaugural Dissertation*, 2.399.4–6

Stuffed September night, the hot leaves bump
on swollen breezes and a fat
black moonlessness.
I got up (3 AM)

to clean the house, there was
so much pressure on it forcing the butt end down.
I scrubbed counters and mopped floors.
I didn't turn the lights on.
Cleaning

in the dark makes a surprise for later. By then
I will have
slept, woke, come striding back
from infuriated interiors—ah
now

recall
I dreamed
of Wordsworth—his little vials,

Wordsworth collected little vials,
had hundreds of them, his sister stored them on shelves in the pantry—
and yes

to inspire me is why
I put in a bit of Wordsworth but then the page is over, he weighs it to the
ground,
the autumn of him soaking my mop purple in the dyes of what's falling
breathless under its own
senses.

GNOSTICISM VI

Walking the wild mountain in a storm I saw the great trees throw their arms.
Ruin! they cried and seemed aware

the sublime is called a "science of anxiety."
What do men and women know of it?—at first

not even realizing they were naked!
The language knew.

Watch "naked" (*arumim*) flesh slide into "cunning" (*arum*) snake in the next
verse.
And suddenly a vacancy, a silence,

is somewhere inside the machine.
Veins pounding.

SEATED FIGURE
WITH RED ANGLE (1988)
BY BETTY GOODWIN

Seated Figure with Red Angle (1988) by Betty Goodwin.

SEATED FIGURE WITH RED ANGLE (1988)
BY BETTY GOODWIN

If body is always deep but deepest at its surface.

If conditionals are of two kinds factual and contrafactual.

If you're pushing, pushing and then it begins to pull you.

If police in that city burnt off people's hands with a blowtorch.

If quite darkly colored or reddish (bodies) swim there.

If afterwards she would sit the way a very old person sits, with no pants on, confused.

If you reach in, if you burrow, if you risk wiping in.

If a point that has been fed over years becomes a little bit alive.

If the seated figure started out with an idea of interrogation.

If there was a quality of very strong electrical light.

If you had the idea of interrogation.

If interrogation is a desire to get information which is not given or not given freely.

If buried all but traceless in the dark in its energy sitting, drifting within your own is another body.

If at first it sounded like rain.

If your defense is perfect after all it was the trees that walked away.

If objects are not solid.

If objects are much too solid.

If there are no faces, if faces are not what you interrogate.

If red makes you think of chance or what chance operates with.

If the feet cross in a way that sucks itself under, sucks analogies (Christ) under.

If as Artaud says anyone who does not smell cooked bomb and condensed vertigo is not worthy of being alive.

If you choose what to undo, if you know how you make that choice.

If you lead her to water.

If you bring her a gift say one of Pascal's thoughts.

If you bring "infinite fractions of solitude" (Nabokov).

If you bring a bit of Artaud like "all writing is shit all writers are pigs."

If conditionals are of two kinds possible and impossible.

If she slides off, if you do.

If red is the color of cliché.

If red is the best color.

If red is the color of art pain.

If Artaud is a cliché.

If artists tell you art is *before thought.*

If you want to know things like where that leg is exactly.

If the horses were exhausted.

If she begged, if she came to the table, if the sequence doesn't matter.

If it begins, a trickle, this thin slow falling of the mind.

If you want to know why the sliding affects your nerves.

If you want to know why you cannot reach your own beautiful ideas.

If you reach instead the edge of the thinkable, which leaks.

If you stop the leaks with conditionals.

If conditionals are of two kinds real and unreal.

If nothing sticks.

If she waits alongside her.

If Miroslav warned us that experimental animals should not be too intelligent.

If to care for her is night.

If an enigma came into the room.

If all the other enigmata fought to get out.

If outside of here the light has gone from the tops of the trees that rise over a brick wall opposite.

If conditionals are of two kinds now it is night and all cats are black.

If how many were killed by David exceeds how many were killed by Saul by tens of thousands.

If they don't feel pain the way we do.

If you drove here with toys in the backseat.

If you wrote a word on the floor of the cell in waterdrops and videotaped it drying.

If Vitruvius says no temple can be coherently constructed unless it is put together exactly as a human body is.

If red is the color of italics.

If italics are a lure of thought.

If Freud says the relation between a gaze and what one wishes to see involves allure.

If you cannot remember what word you wrote.

If art is the servant of allure.

If Vitruvius does not talk about taking temples apart but we may assume the same canon applies.

If there is no master of allure.

If conditionals are of two kinds allure and awake.

If no matter how you balance on the one you cannot see the other, cannot tap the sleep spine, cannot read what that word was.

If "contrafactual" applied to conditionals means the protasis is false.

If (for example) "had you not destroyed the barometer it would have forewarned us" implies that we are now standing in a storm of rain.

If as a matter of fact it is a clear night I would say almost relentlessly clear.

If conditional comes between condiment and condolence.

If you do not want to remember what word it was.

If your life bewilders you (*sly life*).

If the rain lashes your face like manes of all the horses of this century.

If conditonals are of two kinds graven and *where is a place I can write this.*

LOTS OF GUNS

An Oratorio for Five Voices[1]

OPENING GUN DIALOGUE

[all snap flags]
Who are you?
A stranger.
Why are you here?
To take your life and stuff it in a box.
You have no right.
My gun gives me the right.
I veto your gun.
Your veto is unreasonable.
Your reason is a mystery.
Your mystery is a way of lying.
This concept is no longer in use.
You mean lying?
The concept of lying, yes, is no longer in use.
What do you do when you want to avoid telling the truth?
I use a microwave oven.
How does that work?
Has 600 watts and 5 power levels.
Isn't it hard on your gun?
I never put my gun in the microwave—there is no need. Guns do not lie.

[chorus]
The mythic past.
The curious past.
The man has the wound.
The woman has the gun.
The mythic past.
The curious past.
Lots of guns against the wall.
Lots of guns in the usual world.
The man is conscious.
The woman disastrous.
The mythic past.
The curious past.
Wasn't it here
by the lonesome pine
you carved your name and I carved mine?
O Alice!
O Alice!
I'm blue for you
like the lonesome pine.

GUNS AND DESIRE I

[all snap flags]
What does it matter to me that there were other people to love?

GUNS AND DESIRE II

[all snap flags]
But all the same one day I heard her talking to her six-year-old little boy and saying you are a good little boy, yes mother he said and you love your mother very much, yes mother he said and you will grow up loving your mother she said, yes mother he said and then you will leave me for a woman will you not, yes mother he said.

LINNAEUS ON GUNS

[all snap flags]
The skin covering our guns is composed of the most splendid fibers, interwoven and everywhere strewn with blood vessels and nerve endings in a remarkable way. Gun skin can be stretched miraculously and then tightened again.

GUNS AND DESIRE III

[all snap flags]
A horrific and violent ransacking of gun body by gun body will unavoidably occur. This is not what a gun actually wants but rather to cling to each syllable without ever having to hear the entire sentence come and go. Come and go are sadly linked are they not. That is the gun condition. Is this condition improved by making love to your gun while it is asleep? Or by absence? Or by neglect? Surely you will desire your gun more the more it forgets your existence, the more it flicks its ears and returns to feeding on the lower willow branches.

[chorus]
The mythic past.
The curious past.
Lots of guns expressing restlessness.
Lots of guns with cherry cobbler.
The man is tremendously.
The woman almost.
The mythic past.
The curious past.
Lots of guns in a manner.
Lots of guns really would have.
I am so glad you like adverbs.
In the pale moonshine
our hearts entwine.
I pledged my love

and you pledged thine.
Now I'm blue for you
like the lonesome pine.

THE PRESOCRATIC PROBLEM

[all snap flags]
Parmenides named his gun The Hot Power of the Stars. His gun was one, uncreated, imperishable, timeless, changeless, perfect, spherical. Spherical was the problem.

AN OLD HYPOTHESIS

[all snap flags]
God is to be believed in so far as he speaks of his gun.

GUNS AND ROBBERY

[all snap flags]
"Quotations in my writing," said Walter Benjamin on page 570 of volume 1 of his *Collected Works,* "are like robbers by the roadside who make an armed attack and

relieve the idle passerby of his convictions." Meanwhile in Washington, D.C., no one is surprised anymore by a break-in. They just hope they get a "clean" robber—one who takes the jewels and electronics without shitting on the rug.

[chorus]
The mythic past.
The curious past.
The man orders beef.
The woman pork.
Here comes Death
beating his fork.
Lots of guns, that's the basis.
Lots of guns, that's the trick.
The man has a theory.
The woman has hipbones.
Here comes Death.
How sentimental.
O Alice!
O Alice!
You carved your name
and I carved mine.
Now I'm blue for you
like the lonesome pine.

VIA NEGATIVA

[all snap flags]
In ancient Chinese tradition (I have heard) there is a genre of poems written by ghosts. For ghost authors the gun is a line that separates this from that, left from right, too much from too little, and it is neither the one nor the other but possesses the blackness of both. A blackness in which I am suspended, you are suspended, and its water is sold for mirrors. Ghosts are distinguishable from regular people by their gliding walk, apparently on no feet.

TENDER GUNS

[all snap flags]
The archaeology of Troy is an archaeology of guns, for all the guns in the world have come to Troy, all the guns ever invented were invented for Troy. Guns are the red and tender habit of Troy. So Homer begins the sixth book of the *Iliad* with fourteen slaughtered Trojans. One after the other each is named and cut down. Then the pattern changes. Menelaos decides to take Adrastos alive. Simple reason: rich father, big ransom. Adrastos promises bronze and iron and gold. *Okay,* says Menelaos. Momentarily things look good for Adrastos. Then Agamemnon runs up screaming. *No, you weakling! Let none of them escape, let not one of them live, not even the infant thing in the womb of its mother! Let every last Trojan perish out of Troy into careless oblivion, unhoused, unfuneralled and blotted out!* So noble Agamemnon spoke and he drove his gun into Adrastos, into the soft part of the

body that lies between the rib and the hip and then, turning him over, he put his heel on the chest of Adrastos and drew out the glorious gleaming great-hearted gun and Adrastos' soul came with it.

CLOSING GUN DIALOGUE

[all snap flags]
What are you doing?
Calling the police.
Why?
To give them a description of your gun.
How do you describe it?
Thin, dark, rather nervous, almost birdlike.
You have entirely misunderstood my gun.
Do you want to talk to the police yourself?
No.
Then be quiet.
My gun is not nervous! My gun is not birdlike!
Sit down please.
My gun is on continuous alert status!
I charge you with plotting against the state, you and your gun too—no distinction between principal and accessory, all involved are sentenced to death by slicing. And your entire household including nonmourning relatives to be forfeit to

the government.

Asymmetric response!

Yes well I have no choice. Our temples are at stake. Our nutmeg is at stake.

Once again it all comes down to nutmeg!

God promised us that nutmeg is our truth.

Other spices exist.

That is not the point.

I've lost track of the point.

Further evidence of your sedition.

You are arguing in a circle.

You gun people always say that.

What are you doing now?

Putting the phone in the microwave.

Can I make a call first?

No.

I get one call, it's the law.

That law doesn't apply to cases of microwave or to killings classed as "accidental."

Accidental?

"Accidental" means what ear and eye do not reach, what thought and care do not reach, as when one is shooting wild animals or for some reason throwing bricks or tiles off a roof and a person gets hit.

What will you do with my gun after I am accidentally killed?

We welcome your suggestions on that.

Well I have a son who needs a gun.

Good. We'll sell it back to him.
He is very poor.
We have several payment plans.
Speech fails me now.
God have mercy on you.

[chorus]
In the pale moonshine
our hearts entwine,
you love your gun and I love mine.
Like the mountains I'm blue.
Like the pine I'm so lonesome for you.
Tender guns.
Tender guns.
Tender
guns.

1. *Lots of Guns,* originally composed as a contribution to a "Tribute to Gertrude Stein" organized by Susan Sontag for Pen American Center, had its debut at the Donnell Library in New York City in March 2003 with five performers, including me. The text was mainly spoken, with italicized portions sung *a capella* to the tune of "On the Trail of the Lonesome Pine," allegedly Gertrude Stein's favorite song. Performers were equipped with a triangular white paper flag on a long stick, held parallel to the right leg then snapped smartly up and down once, by all in unison, to mark the start of each section. Savitri Durkee directed the production with characteristic crackle.

QUAD

As clear marks go these are experts.

QUAD [1]

how does it begin

Begins on a thinness—thin as the plate of reality that you climb back up over (from behind) when waking out of a too bright dream—and thinly on the plate Beckett has balanced his little factory of clear marks. Clear marks tilt and run on the plate never exasperated, never clumsy, never cruel. All the clear marks that he drained off the exasperated, clumsy, cruel antics of Malone and Molloy and Mildred, of Mag, Moran, Macmann, Mercier, Minnie, Winnie, Worm and Watt and Christ and so on (I guess) ended up here, saved for study, motioned into a picture.

why save clear marks

Better question: does Beckett strike you as a person who ever interrogated his own economic impulses? So once you have decided to save clear marks, you may hope to find yourself "beyond that black beyond" where everything not clear, not marked, just goes away. Going away is key. Even the clear marks seem to be trying to go away.

do they go away

Yes but they come back then go away again and it ends amid exits. It ends in time, I mean stranded.

is there a plot

To keep moving at all times and not touch the hole at the center of the thinness. Each clear mark moves in from a corner of the thinness, (which is rectangular),

119

dodges around the hole, moves out to a different corner of the thinness, paces around the edge to the nearest counter-clockwise corner, moves in from that corner, etc.

what's the hole for
Abgrund ist "E," said Beckett. Don't ask me what E is. He also said "danger zone," quoting one of the actors.

how many marks
From one to four at any given time. They add or subtract themselves in sequence: 1 2 3 4 3 2 1 by exits and entrances: pure *Ringkomposition* like a battle scene in Homer. I am speaking ideally. In fact Beckett starts his sequence at 2 and shuts off the camera before the last exit.

how do they look
No faces just cloaks. Blue red yellow white in *Quadrat I*, all white in *Quadrat II*. They look tense. As clear marks go these are experts. *Some ballet training would be desirable*, said Beckett.

does sex matter
Sex indifferent, said Beckett.

what about music
Hollow tinktonk percussion sounds in *Quadrat I*, synchronized to the move-

120

ments of the clear marks, everything busy as a hedge of crickets: do you know the type of archaic Chinese pottery called "crazed glaze"? Nothing in *Quadrat II* but the shuffle of feet. Brought in his own slippers to get the shuffle right.

big mood swing
The all-white ones go slower, slower, seem sadder, acquire that poached-in-eternity look Beckett has in his last photos.

why white
Beckettpeople call this an accident. Some German technician played back the tape of *Quadrat I* in black & white and Beckett saw it and liked it and wrote *Quadrat II*. You can credit this if you like. But he was always playing with translation wasn't he. And *Endgame* plays back very differently than *Fin de Partie*. His very strong ideas about the difference were already formulated in 1931 when he lectured to students in a Paris lycée on "Racine and the Modern Novel." French is more of a work language than English he told them. "The French, cerebral transmission, statement rare, the English climactory," he said. Most of the students were doing their nails but one of them (Rosie) wrote down everything he said in a small notebook which she was courteous enough to show me. She wrote down his approval of Racine's atmospheric backgrounds and disapproval of Balzac's "floodlit facts." She wrote down a Proustian location "between the incandescent body and the damp body" but didn't catch what he said Proust said was between them. She wrote several times the phrase "integrity of incoherence" and mentioned her sadness that at the end of term he went off thinking himself a bad lec-

turer. He was not, she felt, bad. Pauses came at wrong places in his talk, she was grateful for them. I wish I'd kept in touch with Rosie.

Quadrat quiz
Match each item of Column A
with that item from Column B
which most effectively completes its lessness:

Column A	Column B
nec tecum	what the right hand is doing
Troy	slump cue
three are too few	two are too few

further on danger
There is a "jerky turn" ever repeated by each one who reaches the hole, wavers there, then flicks away. Repeated. They forget. Do they forget? On the other hand they never forget. The danger of forgetting is withheld. I see no danger in it.

do I detect a question of genre
Piece for 4 players, percussion and light, said Beckett.

and the light
Raised frontal, icy and important. Important to him. *If there were only darkness all would be clear. . . . But where we have both dark and light we have also the inex-*

plicable, he said in an interview (1961). I am inclined to take this concretely. After all a "dark" theatre is one where no play is on. But Beckettpeople pounce on such remarks as if they were Catherine pulling feathers out of a pillow in *Wuthering Heights*: "Did he shoot my lapwings, Nelly? Are they red any of them? Let me look!" etc. Soon the down is flying about like snow. Gets the down up like no other, does he not.

how much time passes between Quadrat I and Quadrat II
Hunderttausend Jahre, said Beckett.

how much time passes within Quadrat I and Quadrat II
Hard to say. The clear marks go snooping around until he cuts off the camera. We get a section of time—razored out—but whose.

would you say he thematizes his medium
No he thematizes himself—like Elvis singing "How Great Thou Art" he's a one-man quartet.

Quadrat is a religious work
No.

perhaps an infernal work
No.

simply a game
I do not find games simple.

I mean that a game is pure means
Yet this game serves Beckett's end.

what is it (Beckett's end)
To avoid being asked this question.
To be neither punished nor rewarded.
In translating to a tongue that has no word for "neither" you have to explain it by "don't know which is the way." By none of their ways, by way of not this world, by way from wrong start, etc. Or (Homer might say) *with the leap of evening.*

1. In 1982 Beckett produced *Quadrat I* and *Quadrat II* for Süddeutscher Rundfunk television in Stuttgart. *Quadrat I* is an action using four cloaked figures, light and percussion; *Quadrat II* is a variation on *Quadrat I*. The players pace wordlessly on a grid, each following a particular course. *Quadrat I* was filmed in color, *Quadrat II* in black and white. Later in 1982 *Quadrat 1+2* was transmitted by BBC 2, London. First published as *Quad* by Faber and Faber, London, 1984.

H & A SCREENPLAY

Back lawn, smeared moon.
Abelard stands.
Heloise stands.
Chair (near Heloise).

Abelard: I made Heloise stand up.
Heloise sits down.

               I made Heloise sit down.
Heloise stands up.

               Four minutes to one.
Heloise sits down.

               Start with the bone.
Heloise stands up.

               She couldn't stay.
Heloise sits down.

               She could not go on.
Heloise stands up.

               I made Heloise stand up.
Heloise sits down.

               I made Heloise sit down.
Heloise stands up.

               And moreover I was able
               to quote a variety of scriptures pertaining to this.

This changing of Heloise.
For example
the king's daughter is all glory within. . . .
Can bone be changed?
Yes bone can be changed.
How can bone be changed?
By removing it.

Heloise picks up her chair, walks off, Abelard follows her with his eyes and then yells to the empty lawn.

Scratta! Scruppeda! Strittabilla! Sordida!

SCENE 2

Heloise goes down to hell. Close-up on Heloise's face, talking quietly to herself as the world flies past.

Heloise: Hell is nothing unusual.
                 Hell is exactly the same as Heloise's life
                 except
                 no Abelard.
                 Abelard never existed.
                 Abelard never will exist.
                 Hell you know is outside time.
                 Still the absence of time divides itself perpetually
                 into the one same moment
                 (repeat)—
                 moment of her realizing *no Abelard,* moment
                 which exports his being outward
                 from her idea of it
                 into
                 nothing—one
                 same smooth cold lurch of the rod
                 of her idea
                 into a groove of nothing,
                 (repeat)
                 (repeat)
                 (repeat) although

you might say
that the overall fact of her idea of him constituted
a bit of existence for Abelard right there
no matter how reliably it
inserts itself into the clear plastic cover
of a particular negation (repeat)—a point
Heloise would love to have argued
with the *magister* of Paris himself, whose theory of universals
was a bit of embroidery between them
since earliest days of seduction and study,
had he existed—
Lurch.
Click.
Film this however you like.
Important to make it look different from the following
scene
where Heloise returns from hell to her
same life.
How to subtract hell:
faintly.

SCENE 3

Heloise goes down to hell.

We see her appear at an upper window,
step out and sheer toward the ground,
her clothes long white gusts around her.
Perhaps she repeats this.
Fade between.

SCENE 4

Heloise returns from hell.

Smell of sidewalks after night rain.
In the windows we see women waiting.
Upstairs are others waiting.
There is a black and white cat who strolls on the sidewalk, stops.

SCENE 5

Heloise and Abelard are parked on the edge of a gravel road, hot night, no wind.

Why do you fight?

To fight.

If it's a reward you want—

No.

Or do I frighten you—

No.

Whatever the case, I take the road that I take.

Can I touch you?

No.

So what now?

Discipline!

Ah.

Contemplation!

Hmm.

Blessed are the ransomed of the living God.

Abelard you dull me. But don't stop.

I shall give you a prayer.

Fine.

Compose a prayer for you.

Do that.

You can repeat it morning and evening.

I'll hide your name in every word.

Just say it.

Okay.

Let us use Psalm 84—

My soul longeth my soul fainteth my heart and my flesh crieth out—

Exactly.

I welcome your healing, Abelard.

You are not incurable.

Do you want me to be someone else.

I want you to be nothing.

Metaphysically difficult.

Heloise don't bait me.

Purple flash bounces through the car.

Lightning! *says Heloise.*

Police! *says Abelard.*

He shoves a pile of books and papers onto her lap and turns to roll down the window on the driver's side.

135

SCENE 6

Frame contains a black steering wheel and two hands in short white gloves.
Voice-over Heloise.

Answer

only

what he asks stay

away

from the

backwall keep low keep

dry keep his respect. Heloise talks

to herself where Heloise has

to where

the soul oh

Heloise

where the

soul with its soft

edges

cuts

into

the

sharp

body.

SCENE 7

Heloise and Abelard at the kitchen table in a slow August kitchen spearing chunks of watermelon from a plate with forks.

Hot day.

It is.

Supposed to be hot tomorrow too.

Really.

Hot as today I bet.

Oh no.

That's what they say.

Hard to imagine.

Couldn't be this hot two days in a row you think.

Well I hope not.

But then why couldn't it.

I don't know.

I mean it's August.

Good point.

The hot season.

True enough.

Like it or not.

Not.

You know I wonder about those leftovers.

What about them.

Will they last.

Last.
In this heat.
Oh.
I wonder.
Well they're in the fridge.
But still.
Do you want any more watermelon.
No go ahead.
Just one piece left.
It's yours.
I love this colour.
You mean watermelon.
Red flesh black seeds.
It's two colours.
Yes.
Hot colours.
No cool.
You think so.
I do.

What Heloise thinks on an ordinary day.

Here comes another blank one.

What Heloise thinks on special days.

How lips work.

SCENE 9

Heloise's motel room (outside the window a Best Western sign) furnished
in tones of beige and brown with red silk pillows here and there.
Heloise is backing away from the door as Abelard enters.
Throughout the first part of this scene Heloise speaks to Abelard (he does not answer) while
holding one of the red silk pillows against her body.

What do you want?

Are you unwell?

Depressed?

Need money?

Have a bad dream?

The room is silent.
A wind moves outside.
The door rustles on its hinge.

Heloise whips the red silk pillow hard at him.
The pillow hits him and falls to the carpet.
He looks at the pillow, bends, picks it up, tosses it back to her.

She holds the pillow a moment.
Whips it at him again.
He bends, recovers and tosses it back.
She whips it at him again.
He tosses it back.
Whips it.
Tosses it.
Whips it.
Tosses it.
Whips it.
Tosses it.
Whips it.
Tosses it.
She screams. Turns away, replaces the pillow on the bed, stands with her back to him.

You always win Abelard : it's not God who wins, but you.

Heloise and Abelard are seated side by side on swings in a playground.

I feel bad.

Why?

Our film is almost over and we haven't explained anything.

It's a documentary.

So?

Has no thesis.

Here I come! *She stretches her arms out straight.* I'm a thesis! *Soars out of frame.*

What did you wish to explain?

The darkness, for one thing.

It's true I don't know how to light a film.

That's an understatement.

Well I grew up in tenements.

Should have shot the film there.

I think the building is gone.

Where was it?

Down by the river.

Really.

It's a skating rink now.

That would have been nice.

You like skating?

I like the sounds the smells.

Me too.

Never got very good though.

Takes practice.

Takes a lot of practice.

Practice with the same partner.

Well yes.

One person has to learn to go backwards all the time.

Don't they each go backwards?

You mean alternately?

Yes going one way then the other.

No there's a turn.

Oh.

They turn and go back.

Oh.

That's why it looks elegant.

I guess I missed the turn.

It's the turn gives it symmetry.

That turn fooled me.

It's quick on skates.

Looks so free.

Heloise.

What?

I have to leave now.

No.

Yes.

The camera is still running.

My time is up.

What shall I—?

Abelard has let go his swing and flies out of the frame without answering.
Heloise continues to swing.

SCENE 11

In the mild dawn a row of women is picking chickpeas on the banks of a river.

Snap snap

go the chickpeas into the little buckets. Women slide forward in river grass with a wet shshshsh. Their bending backs tremble the day. Heloise is last in line. The motion is very small.

Snap snap

a sound falls through that day.
No one approaches on the road, no one departs.

TOTALITY: THE COLOUR
OF ECLIPSE

You might think a total solar eclipse would have no colour. The word "eclipse" comes from ancient Greek *ekleipsis*, "a forsaking, quitting, abandonment." The sun quits us, we are forsaken by light. Yet people who experience total eclipse are moved to such strong descriptions of its vacancy and void that this itself begins to take on colour. What after all is a colour? Something not no colour. Can you make a double negative of light? Would that be like waking from a dream in the wrong direction and finding yourself on the back side of your own mind? There is a moment of reversal within totality. "Reverses Nature," Emily Dickinson mutters.[1] As the moon's shadow passes over you—like a rush of gloom, a tornado, a cannonball, a loping god, the heeling over of a boat, a slug of anaesthetic up your arm (these comparisons occur in the literature)—you will see, through your spectroscope or bit of smoked glass, some of the spectral lines grow lighter, then a flash and the lines reverse—to a different spectrum with some lines removed and others brightened. You are now inside the moon's shadow, which is a hundred miles wide and travels at two thousand miles an hour. The sensation is stupendous. It seems to declare a contest with everything you have experienced of light and colour hitherto. Virginia Woolf, in her essay "The Sun and the Fish" (which records celestial events on 29 June, 1930, at Bardon Fell above Richmond),[2] reads the contest as a race:

> The sun had to race through the clouds and to reach the goal, which was a thin transparency to the right, before the sacred seconds were up.

The race ends in defeat and shows the colours of defeat:

> And as the fatal seconds passed, and we realized the sun was being defeated, had now, indeed, lost the race, all the colour began to go from

the moor. The blue turned to purple; the white became livid as at the approach of a violent but windless storm. Pink faces went green, and it became colder than ever. This was the defeat of the sun.

Hard to know how to go on, after the reversal of colour and defeat of the sun. "This was the end," she says, "the flesh and blood of the world was dead." Other observers of eclipse mention at this instant a feeling of *wrongness*. Emily Dickinson, briefly: "Jehovah's Watch—is wrong!"[3] Annie Dillard, in more detail:

> The sun was going and the world was wrong. The grasses were wrong; they were platinum. . . . This color has never been seen on earth. . . . I was standing in it, by some mistake.

Wrongness has its own color and it is not like anything else. Not even like another eclipse, according to Annie Dillard:

> I had seen a partial eclipse in 1970. A partial eclipse is very interesting. It bears almost no relation to a total eclipse. Seeing a partial eclipse bears the same relation to seeing a total eclipse as kissing a man does to marrying him. . . .[4]

Note the analogy. Drastic analogies abound in the literature of totality; also typical at this blasted moment, to turn to thoughts of kissing and marrying. Many mythological explanations of eclipse involve copulation or the hope of it. For example, old Germanic legend tells how the (male) moon was married to the (female) sun but could not satisfy her fiery passion, he just wanted to go to sleep. They made a bet: whoever woke first in the morning would rule the day. The sun, still turbulent at 4 AM, won the bet but vowed she would not sleep with the moon again. Both of them soon regretted their parting and began to edge toward one another (= eclipse). No sooner do they meet than they fall to quarrelling and go separate ways, the sun bloodred with anger. Historians also like to associate totality with marriage, as in Herodotos' famous account of the eclipse of 585 BC, which took place in the midst of a battle between the Lydians and the Medes. Both armies were so unnerved by the solar situation, they broke off fighting and sealed a truce by arranging nuptials between the daughter of one king and the son of the other.[5] Poets too see a connection between total eclipse and conjugal arrangements. The ancient lyric poet Archilochos mentions totality in a poem of the seventh century BC in which a father disapproves his daughter's marriage plans:

> Nothing in the world [says the father] is astonishing,
> unbelievable or forsworn anymore
> now that Zeus has made night out of noon
> and hidden away the blazing light of the sun . . .[6]

After this the poem becomes fragmentary but the father seems to be using eclipse as an analogy for his daughter's incredible choice of husband. When the poet Pindar witnessed a total eclipse at Thebes (probably in 478 or 463 BC) he put it into his ninth Paean. Pindar's description of "a bright star stolen from the middle of the day" is oddly but dramatically coupled with romantic praise of a Theban nymph named Melia, who "mingled with the god Apollo in her ambrosial bed."[7] But by far the oddest couple in eclipse literature is the one put together by Virginia Woolf in "The Sun and the Fish." This essay indeed is riddled (in several senses) with sex. A bit of cognitive speculation begins it:

> For a sight will only survive in the queer pool in which we deposit our memories if it has the good luck to ally itself with some other emotion by which it is preserved. Sights marry incongruously, morganatically (like the Queen and the Camel), and so keep each other alive. . . . Sights fade and perish and disappear because they failed to find the right mate.

151

Then follows a strong description of total eclipse, which veers off all at once, after totality, to a snapshot of two lizards mating on the path of the Zoological Garden:

> One lizard is mounted immobile on the back of another, with only the twinkle of a gold eyelid or the suction of a green flank to show that they are the living flesh, and not made of bronze. All human passion seems furtive and feverish beside this still rapture.

But she is not content with the rapture of lizards. This immortal moment is immediately married to a third image: that of fish swimming in the tanks of the London Aquarium. The fish are not explained; I've questioned a number of Virginia Woolf experts on this and no one appears to know why she adds fish to lizards. Wouldn't the mental images of eclipse and lizards have made her point and "kept each other alive" (as she says incongruous ideas do, in the queer pool of our mind)? Yet she deliberately complicates this neat union with a third angle of vision. I wonder if third angles were in her mind that day, as she wandered over Bardon Fell in the company of both her husband, Leonard, and her lover Vita Sackville-West. To judge from the observations in her diary (June 30), she was watching Vita all the day, watching Vita with her husband, Harold Nicolson (whom Virginia Woolf elsewhere in her diary describes as "a spontaneous child-like man . . . has a mind that bounces when he drops it"), watching how marriage was going with Vita:

> In our carriage was Vita & Harold, Quentin, Leonard and I. That is Hatfield, I said. I was smoking a cigar. . . . there was one star, over Alexandra Park. Look Vita, that's Alexandra Park, said Harold. The N[icolson]s got sleepy; Harold curled up with his head on Vita's knee. She looked like Sappho by Leighton, asleep; so we plunged through the midlands, made a very long stay at York. Then at 3 we got out our sandwiches, & I came in

from the wc to find Harold being rubbed clean of cream. . . . Then we
had another doze, or the N.'s did. . . .[8]

It was 1930. Marriage was going well with the Sapphic Vita, marriage was going
well with the virginal Virginia. Besides that, they were enjoying their affair, look-
ing forward to spending the weekend after the eclipse together at Long Barn
(Vita's ancestral estate). Still, totality is a phenomenon that can flip one's ratios
inside out. I wonder if they paused to look at each other, these mated and
unmated people, on the exposed plane of an ordinary moment of that curious,
heavy, historic, wrong day. Sudden feeling of oldness. Black upland wind. Bring a
coat, they had been told, and a piece of smoked glass. It will get cold. It will hurt
your eyes. Totality is lightless, and should be colourless, yet may intensify certain
questions that hang at the back of the mind. What is a spouse after all? Will this
one stay, can this one keep me alive?

1. Emily Dickinson, *The Complete Poems*, ed. T. H. Johnson (Boston: Little, Brown, 1958), 415.3.

2. Virginia Woolf, "The Sun and the Fish," in *Collected Essays* (London: The Hogarth Press, 4 vols., 1966–67), 4.519–24.

3. Emily Dickinson, *The Complete Poems*, 415.8.

4. Annie Dillard, *Teaching a Stone to Talk* (New York: Harper & Row, 1982), 89, 91.

5. Herodotos 1.74: *Herodoti Historiae*, ed. C. Hude (Oxford: Oxford Classical Texts, 1908).

6. Archilochos, fragment 74.1–4, in *Greek Lyric Poetry*, ed. D. A. Campbell (Bristol: Bristol Classical Press, 1982).

7. Pindar, *Paeans*, 9.2–3, in *Pindari Carmina cum fragmentis*, eds. B. Snell and H. Maehler (Leipzig: Teubner, 1975), vol. 2.

8. Virginia Woolf, *The Diary of Virginia Woolf*, eds. A. Olivier Bell and A. McNeillie (London: The Hogarth Press, 1980), 3.142.

DECREATION
HOW WOMEN LIKE SAPPHO,
MARGUERITE PORETE AND SIMONE WEIL
TELL GOD

This is an essay about three women and will have three parts. Part One concerns Sappho, a Greek poet of the seventh century BC who lived on the island of Lesbos, wrote some famous poetry about love and is said to have organized her life around worship of the god Aphrodite. Part Two concerns Marguerite Porete, who was burned alive in the public square of Paris in 1310 because she had written a book about the love of God that the papal inquisitor deemed heretical. Part Three concerns Simone Weil, the twentieth-century French classicist and philosopher whom Camus called "the only great spirit of our time."

What if I were to begin an essay on spiritual matters by citing a poem that will not at first seem to you spiritual at all. Fragment 31 of Sappho says:

.   He seems to me equal to gods that man
      whoever he is who opposite you
      sits and listens close
      to your sweet speaking

      and lovely laughing—oh it
      puts the heart in my chest on wings
      for when I look at you, even a moment, no speaking
      is left in me

      no: tongue breaks and thin
      fire is racing under skin
      and in eyes no sight and drumming
      fills ears

      and cold sweat holds me and shaking
      grips me all, greener than grass
      I am and dead—or almost
      I seem to me.

      But all is to be dared, because even a person of poverty . . .[1]

This poem has been preserved for us by the ancient literary critic Longinus, who quotes four complete Sapphic stanzas and then the first line of what looks like a fifth stanza and then breaks off, no one knows why. But the first four stanzas seem to compose a unit of music and thought; let's consider the thought. It comes to us bathed in light but this is the weirdly enclosed light of introspection. Sappho is staging a scenario inside the little theatre of her mind. It appears to be an erotic scenario but the characters are anonymous, their interrelations obscure. We don't know why the girl is laughing, nor what the man is doing there, nor how Sappho's response to them makes sense. Sappho seems less interested in these characters as individuals than in the geometric figure that they form. This figure has three lines and three angles. One line connects the girl's voice and laughter to a man who listens close. A second connects the girl to Sappho. Between the eye of Sappho and the listening man runs a third. The figure is a triangle. Why does Sappho want to stage this figure? Common sense suggests it is a poem about jealousy. "Lovers all show such symptoms as these," says Longinus. So let's think about what the jealousy of lovers is.

The word comes from ancient Greek *zelos* meaning "zeal" or "hot pursuit." A jealous lover covets a certain location at the centre of her beloved's affection only to find it occupied by someone else. If jealousy were a dance it would be a pattern of placement and displacement. Its emotional focus is unstable. Jealousy is a dance in which everyone moves.

Sappho's poem sets the stage for jealousy but she does not dance it. Indeed she seems to forget the presence of her dancing partners entirely after the first stanza and shifts the spotlight onto herself. And what we see in the spotlight is an unexpectedly spiritual spectacle. For Sappho describes her own perceptual abilities (visual, aural, tactile) reduced to dysfunction one after another; she shows us the objects of outer sense emptying themselves; and there on the brightly lit stage at the centre of her perception appears—her own Being: "I am . . . ," she says at verse 15 ("greener than grass I am").

This is not just a moment of revealed existence: it is a spiritual event. Sappho enters into ecstasy. "Greener than grass I am . . . ," she says, predicating of her own Being an attribute observable only from outside her own body. This is the condition called *ekstasis*, literally "standing outside oneself," a condition regarded by the Greeks as typical of mad persons, geniuses and lovers, and ascribed to poets by Aristotle.

Ecstasy changes Sappho and changes her poem. She herself, she says, is almost dead. Her poem appears to break down and stop. But then, arguably, both of them start up again. I say arguably because the last verse of the poem has a puzzling history and is regarded with suspicion by some scholars, although it appears in Longinus and is corroborated by a papyrus. Let us attempt to see its coherence with what goes before.

"All is to be dared because even a person of poverty . . . ," says the last verse. It is a new thought. The content of the thought is absolute daring. The condition of the thought is poverty. I don't want to give the impression that I know what this verse is saying or that I see where the poem is headed from here, I don't. Overall it leaves me wondering. Sappho sets up a scenario of jealousy but that's not what the poem is about, jealousy is just a figure. Sappho stages an event of ecstasy but that's not what the poem is about either, ecstasy is just a means to an end. Unfortunately we don't reach the end, the poem breaks off. But we do see Sappho begin to turn towards it, towards this unreachable end. We see her senses empty themselves, we see her Being thrown outside its own centre where it stands observing her as if she were grass or dead. At which point a speculation occurs to me: granted this is a poem all about love, do we need to limit ourselves to a reading of it that is merely or conventionally erotic? After all, Sappho is believed by some historians to have been not just a poet of love and a worshipper of Aphrodite on Lesbos but also a priest of Aphrodite's cult and a teacher of her doctrines. Perhaps Sappho's poem wants to teach us something about the metaphysics or even the theology of love. Perhaps she is posing not the usual lovesong complaint, *Why don't you love me?* but a deeper spiritual question, *What is it that love dares the self to do?* Daring enters the poem in the last verse when Sappho uses the word *tolmaton*: "is to be dared." This word is a verbal adjective and expresses a mood of possibility or potential. Sappho says it is an *absolute* potential:

> *pan tolmaton*: *all* is to be dared.

Moreover she consents to it—or seems to be on the point of consenting when the poem breaks off. Why does she consent? Her explanation no longer exists. So far as it goes, it leads us back to her ecstatic condition. For when an ecstatic is asked the question, *What is it that love dares the self to do?* she will answer:

> *Love dares the self to leave itself behind, to enter into poverty.*

Marguerite Porete was burned at the stake in 1310 for writing a book about the absolute daring of love. *The Mirror of Simple Souls*[2] is a theological treatise and also a kind of handbook for people seeking God. Marguerite Porete's central doctrine is that a human soul can proceed through seven different stages of love, beginning with a period of "boiling desire,"[3] to an ecstasy in which the soul is carried outside her own Being and leaves herself behind. This departure from her own centre is not passive. Like Sappho, Marguerite first discovers in reality a certain absolute demand and then she consents to it. Like Sappho she sees herself split in two by this consent and experiences it as a kind of "annihilation." Marguerite's reasoning is severe: she understands the essence of her human self to be in her free will and she decides that free will has been placed in her by God in order that she may give it back. She therefore causes her will to depart from its own will and render itself back to God with nothing left over. Here is how she describes this event:

> . . . a ravishing expansion of the movement of divine Light is poured into the Soul and shows to the Will [the rightness of what is . . . in order to move the Soul] from the place where it is now and ought not to be and render it back to where it is not, whence it came, there where it ought to remain. Now the Will sees . . . that it cannot profit unless it departs from its own will. And thus the Soul parts herself from this will and the Will parts itself from such a Soul and then renders itself and gives and goes back to God, there where it was first taken, without retaining anything of its own. . . .[4]

163

Now it is noteworthy, in light of Sappho's account of ecstasy and its consequences, that Marguerite Porete twice refers to herself at the moment when God's abundance overflows her as:

> I who am in the abyss of absolute poverty.[5]

She also describes her impoverishment as a condition of physical and metaphysical negation:

> Now such a Soul is nothing, for she sees her nothingness by means of the abundance of divine understanding, which makes her nothing and places her in nothingness.[6]

Throughout *The Mirror* she speaks of herself as null, worthless, deficient, deprived and naked. But at the same time she recognizes her poverty as an amazing and inexpressible kind of repletion; and of this absolute emptiness which is also absolute fullness she speaks in erotic language, referring to God as "overflowing and abundant Lover" or as "the Spouse of my youth."[7] Even more interesting for our analogy with Sappho, Marguerite Porete twice proposes jealousy as a figure for her relationship with God. Thus she refers to God as "the most high Jealous One" and speaks of God's relation to her Soul in this way:

> Jealous he is truly! He shows it by his works which have stripped me of myself absolutely and have placed me in divine pleasure without myself. And such a union joins and conjoins me through the sovereign highness of creation with the brilliance of divine being, by which I have being which is being.[8]

Here is an unusual erotic triangle consisting of God, Marguerite and Marguerite. But its motions have the same ecstatic effect as the three-person situation in Sappho's poem. Marguerite feels her self pulled apart from itself and thrown into a condition of poverty, to which she consents. Her consent takes the form of a peculiarly intense triangular fantasy:

> . . . and I pondered, as if God were asking me, how would I fare if I knew that he preferred me to love another more than himself? And at this my sense failed me and I knew not what to say. Then he asked me how would I fare if it could happen he should love another more than me? And here my sense failed me and I knew not what to say. . . . Beyond this, he asked me what would I do and how would I fare if it could be he preferred another to love me more than he. . . . And there I fainted away for I could say nothing to these three things, nor refuse, nor deny.[9]

Notice how Marguerite turns the fantasy this way and that, rotating its personnel and reimagining its anguish. Jealousy is a dance in which everyone moves. It is a dance with a dialectical nature. For the jealous lover must balance two contradictory realities within her heart: on the one hand, that of herself at the centre of the universe and in command of her own will, offering love to her beloved; on the other, that of herself off the centre of the universe and in despite of her own will, watching her beloved love someone else. Naked collision of these two realities brings the lover to a sort of breakdown—as we saw in Sappho's poem—whose effect is to expose her very Being to its own scrutiny and to dislodge it from the centre of itself. It would be a very high test of dialectical endurance to be able to, not just recognize, but consent to this breakdown. Sappho seems to be entering on a mood of consent when her poem stops. Marguerite faints three times before she can manage it. But then, with a psychological clarity as amazing as Sappho's, Marguerite pushes open the implications of her own pain. Here is her analysis of what she sees when she looks inside Marguerite:

> And so long as I was at ease and loved myself "with" him, I could not at all contain myself or have calm: I was held in bondage by which I could not move. . . . I loved myself so much along "with" him that I could not answer loyally. . . . Yet all at once he demanded my response, if I did not

want to lose both myself and him. . . . I said to him that he must want to test me in all points.[10]

Marguerite reaches rockbottom here when she faces the fact that loyalty to God is actually obstructed by her love of him because this affection, like most human erotic feeling, is largely self-love: it puts Marguerite in bondage to Marguerite rather than to God. Her reasoning uses the figure of jealousy in two ways. She sees jealousy as an explanation of her own feelings of inner division; she also projects jealousy as a test of her ability to de-centre herself, to move out of the way, to clear her own heart and her own will off the path that leads to God. For in order to (as she says) "answer God loyally" she cannot stay one with her own heart or with her own will, she cannot love her own love or love herself loving or love being loved. And insofar as she can "annihilate" all these—her term—she can resolve the three angles of the dance of jealousy into a single nakedness and reduce her Being from three to two to one:

> Now this Soul . . . has left three and has made two one. But in what does this one consist? This one is when the soul is rendered into the simple Deity, in full knowing, without feeling, beyond thought. . . . Higher no one can go, deeper no one can go, more naked no human can be.[11]

Simone Weil was also a person who wanted to get herself out of the way so as to arrive at God. "The self," she says in one of her notebooks, "is only a shadow projected by sin and error which blocks God's light and which I take for a Being." She had a program for getting the self out of the way which she called "decreation." This word is a neologism to which she did not give an exact definition nor a consistent spelling. "To undo the creature in us" is one of the ways she describes its aim.[12] And when she tells of its method she uses language that may sound familiar. Like Marguerite Porete she expresses a need to render back to God what God has given to her, that is, the self:

> We possess nothing in this world other than the power to say "I." This is what we must yield up to God.[13]

And like Marguerite Porete she pictures this yielding as a sort of test:

> God gave me Being in order that I should give it back to him. It is like one of those traps whereby the characters are tested in fairy tales. If I accept this gift it is bad and fatal; its virtue becomes apparent through my refusal of it. God allows me to exist outside himself. It is for me to refuse this authorization.[14]

And also like Marguerite Porete she feels herself to be an obstacle to herself inwardly. The process of decreation is for her a dislodging of herself from a centre where she cannot stay because staying there blocks God. She speaks of a need "to withdraw from my own soul" and says:

167

God can love in us only this consent to withdraw in order to make way for him.[15]

But now let us dwell for a moment on this statement about withdrawal and consent. Here Simone Weil enters upon a strangely daring and difficult negotiation that seems to me to evoke both Marguerite Porete and Sappho. For Simone Weil wants to discover in the three-cornered figure of jealousy those lines of force that connect a soul to God. She does not, however, fantasize relationships with ordinary human lovers. The erotic triangle Simone Weil constructs is one involving God, herself and the whole of creation:

> All the things that I see, hear, breathe, touch, eat; all the beings I meet— I deprive the sum total of all that of contact with God, and I deprive God of contact with all that insofar as something in me says "I." I can do something for all that and for God—namely, retire and respect the *tête-à-tête*. . . .

> I must withdraw so that God may make contact with the beings whom chance places in my path and whom he loves. It is tactless of me to be there. It is as though I were placed between two lovers or two friends. I am not the maiden who awaits her betrothed but the unwelcome third who is with two betrothed lovers and ought to go away so that they can really be together.

> If only I knew how to disappear there would be a perfect union of love between God and the earth I tread, the sea I hear. . . .[16]

If only she could become what Marguerite Porete calls an "annihilated soul," if only she could achieve the transparency of Sappho's ecstatic condition "greener than grass and almost dead," Simone Weil would feel she had relieved the world of an indiscretion. Jealousy is a dance in which everybody moves because one of

168

them is always extra—three people trying to sit on two chairs. We saw how this extra person is set apart in Marguerite Porete's text by a canny use of quotation marks: remember her plaintive observation:

> I loved myself so much along "with" him that I could not answer loyally.[17]

When I read this sentence the first time, it seemed odd to me that Marguerite Porete puts the quotation marks around the "with" rather than around one of the pronouns. But Marguerite knows what she is doing: the people are not the problem here. Withness is the problem. She is trying to use the simplest language and the plainest marks to express a profoundly tricky spiritual fact, viz. that I cannot go towards God in love without bringing myself along. And so in the deepest possible sense I can never be alone with God. I can only be alone "with" God.

To catch sight of this fact brings a wrench in perception, forces the perceiver to a point where she has to disappear from herself in order to look. As Simone Weil says longingly:

> If only I could see a landscape as it is when I am not there. But when I am in any place I disturb the silence of heaven by the beating of my heart.[18]

As we saw, Marguerite Porete found a way to translate the beating of her own heart into a set of quotation marks around the word "with." And Sappho found a way to record the beating of her heart while imagining its absence—for surely this is the function performed in her poem by "the man who opposite you sits and listens close." This man, Sappho tells us, is "equal to gods"; but can we not read him as her way of representing "the landscape as it is when I am not there"? It is a landscape where joy is so full that it seems to go unexperienced. Sappho does not describe this landscape further but Marguerite Porete offers an amazing account of a soul in some such condition:

> Such a Soul . . . swims in the sea of joy—that is in the sea of delights flowing and streaming from the Divinity, and she feels no joy for she herself is joy, and swims and floats in joy without feeling any joy because she inhabits Joy and Joy inhabits her. . . .[19]

It seems consistent with Simone Weil's project of decreation that, although she too recognizes this kind of joyless joy, she finds in it not an occasion of swimming but one of exclusion and negation:

> Perfect joy excludes even the very feeling of joy, for in the soul filled by the object no corner is left for saying "I."[20]

PART FOUR

Inasmuch as we are now entering upon the fourth part of a three-part essay, we should brace ourselves for some inconsequentiality. I don't feel the cause of this inconsequence is me. Rather it originates with the three women we are studying and the cause of it is the fact that they are writers. When Sappho tells us that she is "all but dead," when Marguerite Porete tells us she wants to become an "annihilated soul," when Simone Weil tells us that "we participate in the creation of the world by decreating ourselves," how are we to square these dark ideas with the brilliant self-assertiveness of the writerly project shared by all three of them, the project of telling the world the truth about God, love and reality? The answer is we can't. It is no accident that Marguerite Porete calls her book a *Mirror*. To be a writer is to construct a big, loud, shiny centre of self from which the writing is given voice and any claim to be intent on annihilating this self while still continuing to write and give voice to writing must involve the writer in some important acts of subterfuge or contradiction.

Which brings us to contradiction and its uses. Simone Weil speaks plainly about these:

> Contradiction alone is the proof that we are not everything. Contradiction is our badness and the sense of our badness is the sense of reality. For we do not invent our badness. It is true.[21]

To accept the true badness of being human is the beginning of a dialectic of joy for Simone Weil:

If we find fullness of joy in the thought that God is, we must find the same fullness in the knowledge that we ourselves are not, for it is the same thought.[22]

Nothing and something are two sides of one coin, at least in the mind of a dialectician. As Marguerite Porete puts it:

Nothing is nothing. Something is what it is. Therefore I am not, if I am something, except that which God is.[23]

She also says:

Lord you are one goodness through opened out goodness, absolutely in you. And I am one badness through opened out badness, absolutely in me.[24]

Marguerite Porete's vision is dialectical but it is not tragic: she imagines a kind of chiastic immersion or mutual absorption by means of which these two absolute opposites—God and the soul—may ultimately unite. She uses various images of this union, for example, iron, which when placed in the furnace actually becomes fire; or a river that loses its name when it flows into the sea.[25] Her common images carry us beyond the dialectical account of God and soul. For dialectic is a mode of reasoning and an application of the intellectual self. But the soul that has been driven by love into God, the soul consumed as into fire, dissolved as if into water—such a soul has no intact intellect of the ordinary human kind with which to construe dialectical relationships. In other words such a soul passes beyond the place where she can *tell* what she knows. To tell is a function of self.

This situation is a big problem for a writer. It is more than a contradiction, it is a paradox. Marguerite Porete broaches the matter, early in her *Mirror,* with her usual lack of compromise:

For whoever talks about God. . . must not doubt but must know without doubt . . . that he has never felt the true kernel of divine Love which makes the soul absolutely dazzled without being aware of it. For this is the true purified kernel of divine Love which is without creaturely matter and given by the Creator to a creature *and takes away absolutely the practice of telling.*[26]

Marguerite delivers herself of a writerly riddle here. No one who talks about God can have experienced God's Love, she asserts, because such Love "takes away absolutely the practice of telling." She reinforces this point later by arguing that, once a soul has experienced divine Love, no one but God ever understands that soul again (chapters 19 and 20). We might at this point be moved to question what Marguerite Porete thinks she is doing in the remaining chapters of her book, which number 139 in all, when she gives a step-by-step account of the soul's progress towards annihilation in God. We might wonder what all this telling is about. But we are unlikely to receive an answer from Marguerite Porete herself. Nor I think will any prudent writer on matters of God and soul venture to nail such things down. Quite the contrary, to leave us in wonder is just what such a writer feels compelled to do. Let us look more closely at how this compulsion works. We have said that telling is a function of self. If we study the way these three writers talk about their own telling, we can see how each of them feels moved to create a sort of dream of distance in which the self is displaced from the centre of the work and the teller disappears into the telling.

Let's begin with Simone Weil, who was a practical person and arranged for her own disappearance on several levels. Among other things, she is believed to have hastened her own death from tuberculosis in 1943 by a regime of voluntary self-starvation undertaken out of sympathy for people in France who didn't have enough to eat. However that may be, when her parents insisted on fleeing France for America in 1942 she briefly and reluctantly accompanied them, leaving behind in the hands of a certain Gustave Thibon (a farmer in whose vineyard she had been working) about a dozen notebooks of personal reflection (which now form a substantial part of her published work). She told him in a letter to use the thoughts in the notebooks however he liked:

> So now they belong to you and I hope that after having been transmuted within you they will one day come out in one of your works. . . . I should be very happy for them to find a lodging beneath your pen, whilst changing their form so as to reflect your likeness. . . .

> In the operation of writing, the hand which holds the pen and the body and soul attached to it are things infinitely small in the order of nothingness.[27]

Gustave Thibon never saw Simone Weil again, nor did he follow the instructions of this letter, to transmute her ideas into his own—at least not explicitly. Instead he went through the notebooks, extracted punchy passages, grouped these under headings like The Self, The Void, The Impossible, Beauty, Algebra, Luck, The Meaning of the Universe, and published them as a book with her name on the title page as its author.[28] That is, he made a serious effort to force her back into the centre of herself, and the degree to which she nonetheless eludes this reinstallation is very hard for readers like you or me to judge from outside. But I admire the final, gentle piece of advice that she gives to him at the close of her letter of 1942:

> I also like to think that after the slight shock of separation you will not feel any sorrow about whatever may be in store for me and that if you should happen sometimes to think of me you will do so as one thinks of a book read in childhood. . . .[29]

When I think of books read in childhood they come to my mind's eye in violent foreshortening and framed by a precarious darkness, but at the same time they glow somehow with an almost supernatural intensity of life that no adult book could ever effect. I remember a little book of *The Lives of the Saints* that was given to me about age five. In this book the various flowers composing the crowns of the martyrs were so lusciously rendered in words and paint that I had to be restrained from eating the pages. It is interesting to speculate what taste I was expecting from those pages. But maybe the impulse to eat pages isn't about taste. Maybe it's about being placed at the crossing-point of a contradiction, which is a painful place to be and children in their natural wisdom will not consent to stay there, but mystics love it. So Simone Weil:

> Man's great affliction, which begins with infancy and accompanies him till death, is that looking and eating are two different operations. Eternal beatitude is a state where to look is to eat.[30]

Simone Weil had a problem with eating all her life. Lots of women do. Nothing more powerfully or more often reminds us of our physicality than food and the need to eat it. So she creates in her mind a dream of distance where food can be enjoyed perhaps from across the room merely by looking at it, where desire need not end in perishing, where the lover can stay, at the same time, near to and far from the object of her love.

Food and love were analogous contradictions for Simone Weil. She did not freely enjoy either of them in her life and was always uneasy about her imaginative relationship to them. But after all, eternal beatitude is not the only state where to look is to eat. The written page can also reify this paradox for us. A writer may *tell* what is near and far at once.

And so, for example, in Marguerite Porete's original terminology the writer's dream of distance becomes an epithet of God. To describe the divine Lover who feeds her soul with the food of truth, Marguerite Porete invents a word: *le Loing-prés* in her Old French, or *Longe Propinquus* in the Latin translation: English might say "the FarNear." She does not justify this word, simply begins using it as if it were self-evident in Chapter 58 of her book, where she is telling about anni-hilation. At the moment of its annihilation, she says, God practices upon the soul an amazing act of ravishing. For God opens an aperture in the soul and allows divine peace to flow in upon her like a glorious food. And God does this in his capacity as *le Loingprés,* the FarNear:

> For there is an aperture, like a spark, which quickly closes, in which one cannot long remain. . . . The overflowing from the ravishing aperture makes the Soul free and noble and unencumbered [and its] peace lasts as long as the opening of the aperture. . . . Moreover the peace is so deli-cious that Truth calls it glorious food. . . .
>
> And this aperture of the sweet movement of glory that the excellent FarNear gives is nothing other than a glimpse which God wants the soul to have of her own glory that she will possess without end.[31]

Marguerite Porete's concept of God as "the excellent FarNear" is a radical inven-tion. But even more radical is the riddle to which it forces her:

> . . . where the Soul remains after the work of the Ravishing FarNear, which we call a spark in the manner of an aperture and fast close, *no one could believe . . . nor would she have any truth who knew how to tell this.*[32]

Inside her own telling Marguerite Porete sets up a little ripple of disbelief—a sort of distortion in the glass—as if to remind us that this dream of distance is after all just a dream. At the end of her book she returns to the concept one last time, say-ing simply:

> His Farness is the more Near.[33]

I have no idea what this sentence means but it gives me a thrill. It fills me with wonder. In itself the sentence is a small complete act of worship, like a hymn or a prayer. Now hymns and prayers are the conventional way for lovers of God to mark God's FarNearness, for prayer lays claim to an immediate connection with this Being whose absence fills the world. But Marguerite Porete was a fairly unconventional lover of God and did not engage in prayer or credit its usefulness. Simone Weil, on the other hand, although she was never a Christian herself, had a profound attachment to that prayer Christians call the Our Father. During the summer of 1941 when she worked in the vineyard of Gustave Thibon she found herself repeating this prayer while she worked. She had never prayed before, she acknowledges in her notebook, and the effect was ecstatic:

> The very first words tear my thoughts from my body and transport it to a place outside space . . . filling every aspect of this infinity of infinity.[34]

Prayer seems to have been for her an experience of spatial contradiction—or perhaps a proof of the impossible truth of God's motion. In another passage she returns to the Lord's Prayer and its impossible truth:

> *Our Father who art in heaven.* There is a sort of humour in that. He is your Father, but just try going to look for him up there! We are quite as incapable of rising from the ground as an earthworm. And how should he for his part come to us without descending? There is no way of imagining a contract between God and man which is not as unintelligible as the Incarnation. The Incarnation explodes unintelligibility. It is an absolutely concrete way of representing impossible descent. Why should it not be the truth?[35]

Why should the truth not be impossible? Why should the impossible not be true? Questions like these are the links from which prayers are forged. Here is a prayer of Sappho's which will offer us one final example of the dream of distance in which a writer tells God:

> . . . [come] here to me from Krete
> to this holy temple where is
> your graceful grove of apple trees and altars
> smoking with frankincense.
>
> And in it cold water makes a clear sound through apple branches
> and with roses the whole place
> is shadowed and down from radiant-shaking leaves
> sleep comes dropping.
>
> And in it a horse meadow has come into bloom
> with spring flowers and breezes
> like honey are blowing. . . .
>
> In this place you Kypris having taken up
> in gold cups delicately
> nectar mingled with festivities:
> pour.[36]

This fragment was scratched on a shard of pottery by a careless hand in the third century BC. The text is corrupt and incomplete. Nonetheless we can identify it as a hymn of the type called "kletic," a calling hymn, an invocation to God to come from where she is to where we are. Such a hymn typically names both of these places, setting its invocation inbetween in order to measure the difference—a difference which it is the function of the hymn to *decreate*—not to destroy, but to decreate. Among the remarks on decreation in Simone Weil's notebooks is the statement:

God can only be present in creation under the form of absence.[37]

For the writer of a kletic hymn, God's absence is something tricky, perhaps impossible, to tell. This writer will have to invoke a God who arrives bringing her own absence with her—a God whose Farness is the more Near. It is an impossible motion possible only in writing. Sappho achieves it by various syntactic choices: for example, suppression of the verb in the first stanza of her poem. In my translation I supply an imperative "Come!" in square brackets as the first word of the poem, and the sense may seem to require this, but the Greek text has no such verb. It begins with the adverb "Here." In fact the imperative verb for which the entire poem, with its slow and onomatopoeically accumulating clauses, seems to be waiting does not arrive until the very last word of our text: "Pour!" The effect of this suspension is uncanny: as if the whole of creation is depicted waiting for an action that is already perpetually *here*. There is no clear boundary between far and near; there is no climactic moment of God's arrival. Sappho renders a set of conditions that at the beginning depend on Aphrodite's absence but by the end include her presence. Sappho imitates the distance of God in a sort of suspended solution—and there we see Divine Being as a dazzling drop that suddenly, impossibly, saturates the world.

To sum up. Each of the three women we've been considering had the nerve to enter a zone of absolute spiritual daring. Each of them undergoes there an experience of decreation, or so she tells us. But the telling remains a bit of a wonder. Decreation is an undoing of the creature in us—that creature enclosed in self and defined by self. But to undo self one must move through self, to the very inside of its definition. We have nowhere else to start. This is the parchment on which God writes his lessons, as Marguerite Porete says.

Marguerite's parchment burned in 1310. To us this may seem an outrage or a mistake. Certainly the men who condemned her thought she was all wrong and referred to her in the proceedings of her trial not only as "filled with errors and heresies" but as *pseudo-mulier* or "fake woman."[38]

Was Marguerite Porete a fake woman?

Society is all too eager to pass judgments on the authenticity of women's ways of being but these judgments can get crazy. As a case in point, the book for which Marguerite Porete was burned in 1310 was secretly preserved and copied after her death by clerics who transmitted the text as an anonymous devotional work of Christian mysticism, until 1946 when an Italian scholar reconnected the *Mirror* with the name of its author. At the same time, it is hard to commend moral extremism of the kind that took Simone Weil to death at the age of thirty-four; saintliness is an eruption of the absolute into ordinary history and we resent that. We need history to remain ordinary. We need to be able to call saints neurotic, anorectic, pathological, sexually repressed or fake. These judgments sanctify our own survival. By the same token, Sappho's ancient biographers tried to discredit her seriousness by assuring us she lived a life of unrestrained and incoherent sexual indulgence, for she invented lesbianism and then died by jumping off a cliff for love of a young man. As Simone Weil says:

Love is a sign of our badness.[39]

Love is also a good place to situate our mistrust of fake women. What I like best about the three women we've been studying is that they know what love is. That is, they know love is the touchstone of a true or a false spirituality, that is why they play with the figure of jealousy. As fake women they have to inhabit this figure gingerly, taking a position both near and far at once from the object of their desire. The truth that they tell from this paradoxical position is also fake. As Marguerite says briskly:

For everything that one can tell of God or write, no less than what one can think, of God who is more than words, is as much lying as it is telling the truth.[40]

So in the end it is important not to be fooled by fake women. If you mistake the dance of jealousy for the love of God, or a heretic's mirror for the true story, you are likely to spend the rest of your days in terrible hunger. No matter how many pages you eat.

1. Sappho, fragment 31, in *Sappho et Alcaeus Fragmenta,* ed. Eva-Maria Voigt (Amsterdam: Standardausgabe, 1971).

2. Marguerite Porete, *Le Mirouer des simples âmes anienties et qui seulement demeurent en vouloir et désir d'amour,* ed. R. Guarnieri = *Archivio Italiano per la Storia della Pietà* 4 (1965), 513–635. The text was composed in Old French; there are two recent English translations which I have consulted and adapted: *Marguerite Porete: The Mirror of Simple Souls,* trans. E. Babinsky (New York: Paulist Press, 1993); *The Mirror of Simple Souls,* trans. E. Colledge, J. C. Marler and J. Grant (Notre Dame, Ind.: Notre Dame Univ. Press, 1999). Henceforth this book = MP.

3. MP, chap. 118.

4. Ibid.

5. MP, chap. 38.

6. MP, chap. 118.

7. MP, chaps. 38, 118.

8. MP, chap. 71.

9. MP, chap. 131.

10. Ibid.

11. MP, chap. 138.

12. Simone Weil, *Gravity and Grace,* trans. A. Wills (Lincoln, Nebraska: Univ. of Nebraska Press, 1997), 81. Henceforth this book = SW. (The translation is somewhat adapted.)

13. Ibid., 71.

14. Ibid., 87.

15. Ibid., 88.

16. Ibid.

17. MP, chap. 131.

18. SW, 89.

19. MP, chap. 28.

20. SW, 77.

21. Ibid., 148.

22. Ibid., 84.

23. MP, chap. 70.

24. MP, chap. 130.

25. MP, chaps. 25, 82.

26. MP, chap. 18, emphasis added. The text of chapter 18 is controversial; the oldest extant manuscript of Marguerite Porete's book in Old French (made about 1450) does not contain the phrase in italics, while an older Latin translation (made about 1350) does. See Paul Verdeyen, "La première traduction latine du *Miroir* de Marguerite Porete," *Ons Geestelijk Erf* 50 (1984), 388–89.

27. SW, 11.

28. Simone Weil, *La pesanteur et la grâce* (Paris: Plon, 1948).

29. SW, 12.

30. SW, 153.

31. MP, 58, 63.

32. MP, 58, emphasis added.

33. MP, 135.

34. Simone Weil, *The Simone Weil Reader,* ed. G. Panichas (New York: David McKay, 1977), 492.

35. SW, 148.

36. Sappho, fragment 2, in *Sappho et Alcaeus Fragmenta,* ed. Eva-Maria Voigt (Amsterdam: Standardausgabe, 1971).

37. SW, 162.

38. Paul Verdeyen, "Le procès d'inquisition contre Marguerite Porete et Guiard Cressonesart (1309–1310)," *Revue d'histoire ecclésiastique* 81 (1986), 47–94.

39. SW, 111.

40. MP, 119.

DECREATION

(An Opera in Three Parts)

PART ONE

Love's
Forgery

CAST: Hephaistos: lame god of the forge and husband of Aphrodite
Aphrodite: goddess of love and wife of Hephaistos
Ares: god of war and lover of Aphrodite
Volcano Chorus: 7 female robots built by Hephaistos to help
him at the forge

ARGUMENT: Jealous of his wife, Aphrodite, who has taken Ares as her lover,
Hephaistos broods darkly in his mind. Since he is god of the forge—god of fire,
art, craft, igneous eruptions and technological cunning—he goes to his work-
shop and fashions a trap out of volcanic chains hammered so thin they are all but
invisible. With the help of his robots he rigs up this trap around the bed (his own
bed!) where Ares and Aphrodite like to mingle in love. Hephaistos hides. Ares and
Aphrodite enter the bed. Kiss, etc. The trap entraps them. Hephaistos emerges
from hiding and exults over the lovers. Rage and exhilaration of Hephaistos. Ares
and Aphrodite begin to bargain lightheartedly with Hephaistos to release them.
Hephaistos' high mood shifts down gradually to sadness as he realizes that by
their lightness they have already won. Hephaistos undoes the trap. Ares and
Aphrodite bound away to perfumed places. Hephaistos disassembles the trap and
lies down in the bed by himself.

MUSIC:

Hunger Tango: Hephaistos considers love's satisfactions
Stroke and Dye Aria: Aphrodite ponders love's frailty
New Chorus: Chorus comment on love's timing
Sugar Aria: Ares celebrates love's warfare
Late Chorus: Chorus comment on love's timing
Bargaining Trio: Ares, Aphrodite and Hephaistos discuss terms of release
Aria of Brittle Failure Theory: Hephaistos and the chorus in a final mind

Hephaistos' Hunger Tango
[sung by Hephaistos alone at the forge at night]

                                        Hunger
                                   looks like me
                          but it is not original with me.
                Hunger sparkles as you know everywhere secretly.
                Daggers, diamonds, prepositions, Aphrodite.
                How I longed
                (I confess)
           to be free.
     So one day
I put a rose in my hair and I asked her and wild swans carried her to me saying *Yes!*
     Likely couple,
                unlikely couple.
                     Why did they marry?
                people said.
                I popped all the corks, the night turned red!
                     But she looked at me sadly when I got into bed.
                                        Wed or unwed
                                             she had for me
                                                  no
                                                  hunger.

So we
got
started.
I didn't know her she
didn't know me.
Isn't that how marriage is supposed to be?
I remember the rose and swans
and how we
rather awkwardly
mingled
then parted.
I'd give that 6 out of 10 said
my
wife
Aphrodite
the
tenderhearted.
I guess I exaggerate
when I say
"got started."

                   Hunger
                stays with me
          but it is not original with me.
        Hunger sleeps in all things mysteriously.
Roses, roses, roses, roses, Aphrodite.
How I long
(I confess)
to
be
free.

Aphrodite's Stroke and Dye Aria
[sung by Aphrodite, waiting by a phone, night]

Because God did not give me good men but rather these wastrels
I was driven
to stroke
the struts of aeroplanes
and other rusty bladelike things on emptied runways horrid for shelter
as I am
and the fantasies kept sending me out those dusty dawns I couldn't find
even a palmful of it
to damp
the tarmac.

Night gives no relief, night installs it and hurts me.
Other women
no doubt
put this to use:
backed-up roses bleed out the ends of my hair—
I beg you
keep looking.
for the logic I could follow
out of
here.

"To think logically is to be perpetually astonished"
said

the saint
before I destroyed her.
The mind *is* the body.
I hate this fact.
I love this hate.
That
for whose want
I dye.

New Chorus : Love Is Always New When It's You
[sung by Hephaistos and his robots as they begin to erect around his marriage
bed a trap of many fine volcanic chains]

H: Love is always new when it's you.
                     When it's you.
                     Love is always new when it's you.

Chorus: Newly caught.
                     Newly watered.
                     Neological.
                     New-born, new-flayed, newly enfranchised, anew, of late.
                     Fresh-curdled.

H: Love is always new
                     when it's you.
                     When it's you.
                     Love is always new when it's you.

Chorus: Newly polished, newly washed, freshly mourned,
                     newly shorn,
                     newly sawn.
                     Neoplastic.
                     Just having run.

H: Always new.
                     Always new.

When it's you when it's you.
Love is always new when it's you.

Chorus: Young youthful early thoughtless strange; revolution, news,
bad things;

                                      nest with young birds,
                                      to be reared
                                      in a nest,
                                      seller
                                      of young birds.

H: Love is always you
when it's new.
When it's you when it's new when it's new when it's you
love is always
always
when it's you.

Chorus: Not previously experienced.
Coming as a surprise, unforseen, frontpage news.
Replacing one that formerly existed.
Fresh.
Raw.

Just smeared.
Lately learned.
Yolk.

H: Love is always when is always you is always
always always always
always
always
always
new.

Ares' Sugar Aria
[sung by Ares in the back of a taxi, night]

It was easy in winter.
It was easy at evening.
It was easy hourly.
Not really.
Easy sugar.

I get my sugar at a hectic nightclub.
I get it suddenly.
My sugar is sheer art.
Not really.
Easy sugar.

It was easy in winter.
It was easy at evening.
It was easy hourly.
Not really.
Easy sugar.

Are you glad sugar.
Are you resisting.
Are you up to your knees.
Not really.
Easy sugar.

197

Is sugar different.
Not only wary.
Not too often please.
Not really.
                    Easy sugar.

You who sadden.
Now burnt.
Now nocturne.
Not really.
                    Easy sugar.

It was easy in winter.
It was easy at evening.
It was easy hourly.
Not really.
                    Easy sugar.

Late Chorus : Love Is Too Late When It's Untrue
[sung by Hephaistos and his robots as they finish constructing the trap
of the bed]

H: Love is too late when it's untrue.
           Love is too late.
           Love is too late.
           Love is too late
           when it's untrue.

Chorus: Lately bought.
           Lately cooked.
           Late-lamenting.
           Late-born, late-gotten, belated, at last, of late.
           Just spoiled.

H: Love is too late
           when it's untrue.
           Way too late.
           to know
           what to do.
           Love is too late
           when it's untrue.

Chorus: Late-breasted, late-bolted, late-bottled, late-booted,
           lately beheaded.
           Later beatified.
           Over the yardarm.

Aged, venerable, latish, slow, obsolete;
well advanced—

H: Love is too late
        when it's untrue.
        Too late to say
        I wish I never
        met you.
        Love is too late when it's untrue.

Chorus: toward reduction to baselevel;
                            greyish or dusty in color;
                                long familiar,
                                used as an intensive,
                                late in the day,
                                late in the season;
                                a prosecution for putting off marriage—

H: Love is too late
        when it's untrue.
        Always already too late
        too little too bad too stale too sad too
        blue
        when it's untrue.

Chorus: beyond the appointed age.
         Late-learned.
         Old in spawning
         (of the needlefish).
         One who stabs
         at night.

H: Love is too late
         when it's untrue.
         When it's unlate
         is true love too.
         Love is when late it's not too true.
         True is too love when late's not you.
         Too true.
         Too you.
         Too true.

Bargaining Trio

[sung by Ares and Aphrodite as they lie trapped in the bed,
Hephaistos standing alongside]

A and A:	How much silver how much gold how about five.
H:	How about night and day!
A and A:	How about six.
H:	How about Versailles!
A and A:	How about six and a half.
H:	How about the distance between stars!
A and A:	We'll go to eight.
H:	Go to Mars!
A and A:	Why not be reasonable.
H:	Why not be carbon dioxide!
A and A:	Ten is our last offer.
H:	Ten for tasteless!
A and A:	Last offer.
H:	Ten for tacky triangle!
A and A:	Last offer.
H:	Ten for traduced by a trollop!
A and A:	Last offer.
H:	Ten for untutored tyrannic turbulence amounting to farce!
A and A:	Last offer.
H:	Ten for why not try transubstantiation!
A and A:	Last offer.
H:	Done.

Aria of Brittle Failure Theory
[sung by Hephaistos lying on his bed amid debris of the trap,
chorus tapdancing slowly around]

Chorus: *Brittle failure* occurs
of course
when stress on a material exceeds its
tensile force

(so scientists say).

Brittle failure theory
should predict
when some quietly oozing volcano
will erupt

in a deadly pyroclastic way.

But with you Hephaistos it's hard to know.
You're strangely slow.

H: My theory is
I could split my heart on the anvil
and put her inside
and weld it together again
then there she'd stay
till the end of time,
there she'd stay

in no one's heart
but mine.
And I know
our love would grow
freer and brighter
with every stroke of the hammer.

Chorus: *Brittle failure theory* may
in the end fail
to explain how true love can
ever avail

against forgery.

But with you Hephaistos it's hard to know.
You get that strange glow.

H: My theory is
I don't care anymore about justice, injustice,
how they end,
how they start.
I just want to be clear
to be more and more clear
until finally

all you see
is the line
left by the cutting tool
in the heart,
not even
the heart.

PART TWO

Her Mirror of Simple Souls

CAST: Marguerite Porete, mystic and heretic of the 13th century
          God
          Quidnunc Chorus: 15 papal inquisitors

ARGUMENT: Nothing is known of Marguerite Porete's background or origin. She appears like a stain on the air of mediaeval theology about 1296 as author of a book called *Le Mirouer des simples âmes anienties et qui seulement demourent en vouloir et désir d'amour* (*The Mirror of Simple Souls Annihilated and Those Who Only Live in Longing and Desire of Love*), which provoked the wrath of the papal Inquisition because of its form as well as its content. For Marguerite wrote her *Mirror* in vernacular French—not in Latin, which was the official language for thinking about God. When she was instructed by the Church to stop disseminating her ideas this way Marguerite refused. When she was arrested by the Inquisition and told to answer questions about her amazing, inebriated book Marguerite refused. When she was required by the Inquisition to vow she would not teach or publish ever again Marguerite refused. When she was ordered to recant her refusal on pain of death Marguerite refused. Marguerite's trial for heresy took place during the spring of 1310. At noon on June 1 of that year she was burned to death in the public square of Paris.

MUSIC:

Song of the Most High Jealous One: Marguerite tells how it goes with God

Swimming Aria: Marguerite rejoices in the life of the soul

Why Latin: The Quidnunc Chorus worry

Aria of the Trial: Marguerite tells of her trial for heresy

Chorus of the 33 Questions (I and II): The Quidnunc Chorus interrogate Marguerite

Duet of Outer and Inner Space: Marguerite pains herself meditating on the love of God

Aria of the Flames: Marguerite goes free

Song of the Most High Jealous One
[sung by Marguerite and rotating triangles of the Quidnunc Chorus]

M: Jealous he is truly!
           For he has stripped me
           from myself
           absolutely
           and placed me in divine pleasure without myself!

QC: *Defecta,*
           dubia,
           perniciosa est.
           Quis scit?
           Nemo scit.
           Ratio non est.

M: Jealous he is truly!
           For he has disrobed me
           of myself
           absolutely
           and clothed me in divine nakedness without a self!

QC: *Vae te, blanditia!*

M: Jealous he is truly!
           For he has burned me
           out of myself
           absolutely
           and cooled me in divine waters that do not taste of self!

QC: *Bestia,*
        vulgata,
        voluptuosa est.
        Quis laudat?
        Nemo laudat.
        Veritas non est.

M: Jealous he is truly!
        For he has lit me
        within myself
        absolutely
        in a divine night darker than all starless self.

QC: *Vae te, blanditia!*

M: Jealous he is truly!
        For he has parted me
        from myself
        absolutely
        by a ravishing farness nearer than my own self!

QC: *Fabula*
        nefaria
        impiaque est.

Quis saltat?
Nemo saltat.
Sanctitas non est.

M: Jealous he is truly!
          For he has annihilated me
          as myself
          absolutely
          and born me new as nothingness in no self!

QC: *Vae te, blanditia!*

Swimming Aria
[sung by Marguerite]

Soul—
    who is alone in love
        who does nothing for God
            who asks nothing from God
                who hopes nothing of God
                    who cannot be taught
                        who cannot be taken
                  nor given
              nor stolen
        nor won
      nor possessed
    and who possesses
    nothing
    whatsoever
not even joy!
For what burns has no cold
    what swims has no thirst
        and what swims in the sea of joy
                feels no joy
                  for she herself
                          is joy
                    and streams and floats in joy
                as she inhabits joy
        as joy inhabits her
        as flames inhabit fire
        as fire slakes itself—
                Soul:
                swim!

Why Latin
[sung by the Quidnunc Chorus]

Why flesh.
Why standing.
Why Wednesday at noon.

Why not speak Latin.
We have to worry.
Let's worry in Latin.

Whose wisdom.
Whose torture.
Whose young men matter.

This is not Latin.
There are many worries.
Better use Latin.

Will it be wide enough.
Won't you alight.
Would doves do.

Alas for Latin.
Add to our worries
this Latin lack.

Who judges.
Who dabs it.
Who silvers a private life.

Omnes ad unum.
That was Latin!
Here's more:

Quis docet.
Quis nocet.
Quis incensa est.

Lingua Latina
Latina Latina
Latina is best.

Inquisitor doctus
Latinus Latinus
Latinus be blest!

And the fact is
pseudo-mulier
you're under arrest!

Aria of the Trial
[sung by Marguerite]

During my inquisition,
which ran from first of March to last of May 1310,
I heard 33 questions
from the papal inquisitor,
William of Paris,
who had gathered five doctors of law and ten theologians
to consult against my book
(my *Mirror*)
because it contained readable chapters in prose and verse
not to say
errors of heresy! death! sin!
wherefore,
to each of the 33 questions,
notwithstanding they were lively and virtuous questions,
concocted surely by learned men,
who put them to me again and again,
day after day,
worded this way and that way as if I were someone not listening—
to each of these questions I say
I returned
the same glass answer.

I answered nothing.

And like hoarse leaves that crawled along the hissing ground
hotter and faster and faster and faster
until
one day
they lit! under me—

but this is just history: let's have the questions.
Adonc.

Chorus of the 33 Questions (I)
[recitative by the Quidnunc Chorus]

Jesus should be put into a mortar and pounded with a pestle
so much that no one may any longer justly see or taste
the Person put there: do you say this?

Annihilated souls take no account of shame or honour,
ease or pain,
poverty or riches,
hell or paradise or evil or good
or any pious act whatsoever forevermore: do you say this?

Love liberates you from Reason,
love releases you from Obedience,
love replaces the Law,
love commands the Church,
love erases the world and time,
love is a harp of nothingness: do you say this?

Once brought to nothing a soul has no need of Scripture,
of sacraments,
of mass or sermon,
of fasting or prayer,

217

of conscience or rem**o**rse,
of Nature itself **o**r any earthly thing **o**r even sin: do you say this?

Undo virt**u**e! for
unless God sins, the free soul is in no danger of sinning: do you say this?

X marks the place of the soul whose true name is Oblivion: do you say this?

Chorus of the 33 Questions (II)
[sung by the Quidnunc Chorus]

1.	J
2.	J
3.	A
4.	A
5.	A
6.	A
7.	A
8.	A
9.	A
10.	A
11.	A
12.	L
13.	L
14.	L
15.	L
16.	L
17.	L
18.	L
19.	L
20.	L
21.	O
22.	O
23.	O
24.	O
25.	O
26.	O
27.	O
28.	O
29.	O
30.	U
31.	U
32.	X
33.	?

Duet of Outer and Inner Space

[sung by Marguerite Outer, who wears headphones and listens to Marguerite Inner projected behind her on video]

M Inner: And I pondered
as if God were asking me
what would I do and
how would I fare
if I knew
that God preferred me
to love another more than I love God?
And at this my sense failed me and I knew not what to say.
Then God asked me
what would I do and
how would I fare
if I knew
that God preferred
another to love me more than God loves me?
And at this my sense failed me and I knew not what to say.
Beyond this God asked me
what would I do and
how would I fare
if I knew that
it could be
that God preferred
to love another more than me?
And here I fainted dead away
for I could say nothing

to these three things,
neither refuse,
nor deny,
nor ask *Why do you want to test me in all points?*

M Outer [recitative whisper]: It makes me so nervous to listen to it.

Aria of the Flames
[sung by Marguerite]

I am no more in danger of Reason!
     Reason is nothing.
I am no more in danger of Virtue!
     Virtue is nothing.
I am no more in danger of God.
     God has entire need of me—
where else
     can God put
          God's nakedness,
     where else
          can God put
               God's emptiness,
          where else
               can God put
                 God's nothingness,
               where else
                    can God put
                       God's endless end,
                               but
                       in
                me?
          Entire God!
Entire naked empty endlessly ended unmatched God!
Where
       else
          can
               God
                   put
                       God?

PART THREE

Fight Cherries

CAST: Simone Weil: philosopher and mystic
        Madame Weil: mother of Simone
        Monsieur Weil: father of Simone
        Chorus of the Void: 10 transparent tapdancers

ARGUMENT: Simone Weil's life was caught in the net of her parents' care. They cherished, warned, worried, plotted, stocked her fridge, sent her sweaters, followed her to war and transposed her to America (briefly). She took lunges through the net—into Descartes, into Plato, into trade unions and communism and Homer and theology and the arts of hunger. She did not want to be a woman. She wanted to disappear. Certain aspects of disappearance had to be concealed from the parents and so her many letters to them are repetitions of the one same glowingly factitious postcard that every good daughter sends home—*Dear people what splendid weather thanks for the chocolate I'm making lots of friends here kisses to all*—meanwhile she was dying. And when she did die the cable astonished them: her last letter from London had said everything was fine.

MUSIC:

Duet of What Is a Question avec Papa : Simone discusses the void with her father
Chocolate Chorus: Simone and the chorus measure hunger
Duet of the Sleeveless Sports Blouses avec Maman : Simone discusses rules of life with her mother
Decreation Aria: Simone tells the truth about herself
Parental Interlude: M. and Mme Weil construe geometrical possibilities
Aria of Last Cherries: Simone takes her leave

Duet of *What Is a Question* avec Papa
[sung by Simone and Monsieur Weil sitting side by side in armchairs]

M. Weil: What does she mean, void?
            What about shoes and fruits and winecorks, many things exist,
            they have colour and duration, they bear down on us.
            What does she mean?

Simone: Winecorks are not a question.
            Power is a question.
            Not to exercise power is to endure the void.

M. Weil: *Oh yes,* she would say in those days.
            Oh yes you will eventually free yourself and she would make
            a horizontal gesture with her hand
            like a referee in football.

Simone: Football is not a question.
            Imagination is a question.
            Imagination, which fills up the void, is essentially a liar.

M. Weil: New Year's Eve 1933 Trotsky came to see us.
            He had read Simone's article denouncing
            the Russian revolution as a joke.
            With wife and bodyguards he spent a comfortable night.

Simone:	Trotsky's night is not a question.
	Hatred is a question.
	Every void not accepted produces bitter hatred.
M. Weil:	New Year's morning Trotsky pomaded his hair and sat back.
	Simone went in to him, loud shouts were heard.
	The kid is holding her own with Trotsky!
	said Mme Trotsky to Mme Weil.
Simone:	Neither Mme Trotsky nor Mme Weil is a question.
	Grace is a question.
	Grace can only enter where there is void to receive it.
M. Weil:	*Your only mission Comrade Weil is your personality!*
	yelled Trotsky, Simone wrote this down.
	After he left she was proud, would point to the chair.
	See that chair?
Simone:	Chairs are not a question.
	Worldly need is a question.
	The world must be somehow a void to have need of God.

M. Weil:	Simone could not tolerate anything flawed—fruit with a spot on it, poor meat, bad logic, synthetic silk.
Simone:	Silk is not a question. Consolation is a question. Let us avoid weeping so as not to be consoled.
M. Weil:	I own a lithograph of Giacometti's woman in a bedroom under a bare bulb. No street, nothing and that light's blackness pouring out the bulb.
Simone:	Bulbs are not a question. To accept a void in oneself is a question. The energy has to come from somewhere else.

Chocolate Chorus

[sung by Simone Weil and the Chorus of the Void]

Chorus: How many chocolates does a hero eat?
Simone Weil: Not many.
Chorus: How many chocolates does a heretic eat?
Simone Weil: Hardly any.
Chorus: How many chocolates does an anarchist eat?
Simone Weil: Even in summer.
Chorus: How many chocolates does a whirlwind eat?
Simone Weil: No big number.

Chorus: What about Karl Marx?
Simone Weil: Not many.
Chorus: Or Adam and Eve?
Simone Weil: Hardly any.
Chorus: George Herbert?
Simone Weil: Even in summer.
Chorus: A Jew in occupied France?
Simone Weil: No big number.

Chorus: How many chocolates does justice eat?
Simone Weil: Not many.
Chorus: How many chocolates does justice eat?
Simone Weil: Hardly any.
Chorus: How many chocolates does justice eat?
Simone Weil: Even in summer.

Chorus:	How many chocolates does justice eat?
Simone Weil:	No big number.
Chorus:	And how much justice does chocolate eat?
Simone Weil:	Chocolate eats till it feels complete—
	summer winter spring fall—
	there seem to be no restrictions at all!
Chorus:	So how much chocolate has chocolate got?
Simone Weil:	A lot.

Duet of the Sleeveless Sports Blouses avec Maman
[sung by Simone and Madame Weil waltzing in an empty factory
while the Chorus of the Void do calisthenics in slow motion]

Simone: *Chère Maman* I have bought two sleeveless sports
blouses Today a street fight between Nazis and
Communists No I was not there! Please send
me *special post* what I asked for last
letter (the Hegel) Kisses

Mme Weil: Do not forget to watch the stove.
Do not forget to eat some meat.
Do not forget your eyeglasses when you go to the war.

Simone: If I cleanse all but work
from my imagination
out goes desire,
out goes disorder,
out goes today tomorrow whereas and why.
Out goes "I"!

Chorus: A sad saint.
An easy saint.
Not really!
Saints are never left altogether
in place
are they.

Simone: *Chère Maman* I asked Hegel to send
              special post kisses what less.
              sleeves I have Communists fight
              blouses last! Please no sports
              today I was bought (between
              two and the Nazis)

Mme Weil: Do not forget to wear a scarf.
              Do not forget the jam I sent.
              Do not forget a nap before you set off for the war.

Simone: As a squirrel turns in its cage,
              as celestial spheres rotate from age to age,
              so we work
              in order to eat,
              so we eat
              in order to work,
              circling towards salvation in a pasty-faced blue-collar rage!

Chorus: A saint out of tune.
              A speck of a saint.
              Not really!

Saints are never left altogether
in place
are they.

Simone: *Chère Maman* I was *special* there I
          bought less Hegel Please Today have
          Nazis send blouses between sports
          I asked what Communists kissed
          me for (two fight sleeves)
          No not last *post*!

Mme Weil: Do not give your lunch away.
           Do not stumble on the stairs.
           Do not insist on telling everyone about the void.

Simone: Hunger enters the body through work.
           Thirst enters the body through work.
           Joy.
           Time.
           Obedience.
           Death
           likewise.
           Only life does not enter the body through work.
           Life is free!

Chorus: A saint by night.
           A saint beset.
           Not really!
           Saints are never left altogether
           in place
           are they.

Simone: No *special Maman* sport to the last
           fight two less
           kiss sleeves Today!
           cher Hegel!

Mme Weil: Do not leave your money lying by the bed.
           Do not run on the mountains when they are icy.
           Do not forget a card to us as soon as you arrive
           at the war.

Simone: I create myself by work.
           Or else I panic—
           that is to say,
           chère Maman out of my way!

Chorus: A saint blue-black.
           A saint double cream.

Not really!
Saints are never left altogether
in place
are they.

Decreation Aria

[sung by Simone alone in an empty place]

I am excess.
    Flesh.
    Brain.
    Breath.
    Creature who
breaks the silence of heaven,
    blocks God's view of his beloved creation
        and like an unwelcome third between two lovers
    gets in the way.
It is creation that God loves—
    mountains and sea and the years after—
        blue simple horizon of all care.
    World as it is when I am not there.
Undo this creature!
    Excess.
    Flesh.
    Brain.
    Breath.
    Creature.
Undo this creature.

Parental Interlude
[spoken by M. and Mme Weil]

M. Weil:	Nonagons are not useful.
Mme Weil:	But a triangle is true!
M. Weil:	Yes true!
Mme Weil:	How true!
M. Weil & Mme Weil:	And very sweetly too!

M. Weil:	Nonagons are loaded with danger.
Mme Weil:	Coming straight at you!
M. Weil:	Nonagons are a theoretic manoeuvre.
Mme Weil:	And ontologically askew!
M. Weil & Mme Weil:	Precious little we could do.
M. Weil & Mme Weil:	How very sweetly true!

M. Weil:	How true!
Mme Weil:	How true!
M. Weil & Mme Weil:	Now the trees are weeping too.
M. Weil & Mme Weil:	And very sweetly too!
M. Weil & Mme Weil:	Can we meditate a few?
M. Weil & Mme Weil:	What a suddenly saintly view.
M. Weil & Mme Weil:	How very sweetly true!

M. Weil:	Nonagons never get naked.
Mme Weil:	But a triangle longs to!

M. Weil:	Nonagons are jealous of everything.
Mme Weil:	Red, black, yellow, violet, tangerine, off-white, lime green or midnight blue!
M. Weil & Mme Weil:	Do our knees know what to do?
M. Weil & Mme Weil:	And very sweetly too!
M. Weil & Mme Weil:	How very sweetly true!

M. Weil:	Nonagons will revert to themselves soon enough.
Mme Weil:	But a triangle grieves for you!
M. Weil & Mme Weil:	Please translate the word *thankyou*.
M. Weil:	Ontologically not new!
Mme Weil:	Theoretically blue!
M. Weil:	Naked as the dew!
Mme Weil:	I'm lime green who are you?
M. Weil:	No idea what to do!
Mme Weil:	Just be glad this song is through!
M. Weil & Mme Weil:	And very sweetly too!

M. Weil:	Nonagons walk away at the end
Mme Weil:	but a triangle breaks in two!
M. Weil & Mme Weil:	Yes true!
	How true!
M. Weil & Mme Weil:	How very sweetly true!

Aria of Last Cherries
[sung by Simone Weil from a hospital bed, the Chorus of the Void
tapdance around her]

Simone: Is it permissible to seek out affliction?
No it is not. Affliction is defined by necessity.
I was afraid this might not happen to me.

Even as a child I feared failing not in my life but in my death.
So I bought helmet and shroud and await my mission.
What I fear most is that tapping sound.

Chorus: Come cherries come.
Come close.
Come tingle.
Come tease a saint.
Come cherries
continue: we'll discover where you sweat.

Simone: Wheat falls on stones
Flesh and blood are jealous of me.
But milk is for children, take it to the children.

Take all my food away, I cannot lift the spoon.
I must finish this letter to my parents
about the blossoms here

in London all is joy and very happy! perfectly happy!
Also I must ask the chaplain of the Free French
whether, despite the fact that I—

Chorus: Come cherries come.
                    Come close.
                    Come tingle.
                    Come tease a saint.
                    Come cherries
                    continue: we'll discover where you sweat.

Simone Weil: —never made nor do I now make any formal request
for baptism, whether, if I were do so
such a request would be granted or denied.

A need to know is not an abstract need.
God may be hidden but the truth is not.
I do not recognize any right of any person or institution on earth

to limit the workings of the intellect
or the illuminations achieved by love.
Yes you may bless me but *take that water away!*

Chorus: Come cherries come.
                      Come close.
                      Come tingle.
                      Come tease a saint.
                 Come cherries
                 continue: we'll discover where you sweat.

Simone: Perhaps I would like some cherries.
                 There is nothing else I want.
                 I study Sanskrit every day in the sanatorium.

                 But it saddened me to see only stones out the window
                 so I lay back
                 and there was a risk there,
                 I lay back in Lethe.

Chorus: Come cherries come.
                      Come close.
                      Come tingle.
                      Come tease a saint.
                 Come cherries
                 come.

LONGING, A DOCUMENTARY

SHOT LIST

1.   Night.
          River.

          SUBTITLE: *It was for such a night she had waited.*

2.   Trunk of her car is open and lit by a funnel of light from the porch.

3.   She loads the trunk: 4 × 6 trays, photographic papers, strobe light. Strobe doesn't fit, she angles it into the backseat.

4.   She is driving, concentrating, empty highway.

          SUBTITLE: *She was not a person who aimed at eventual reconciliation with the views of common sense.*

5.   She is at the river in deep reeds, watching.

6.   She wades along the edge of the river, watching.

7.   Night plucks her, she stumbles, stops.

8.   She is bending beside the car, unpacking trays.

243

9.   She drags the trays through deep reeds toward the river.
       Moon unclouds itself and plunges by.

       SUBTITLE: *Night is not a fact.*

10.   She walks into the river.

       SUBTITLE: *Facts lack something, she thought.*

11.   She positions the big trays on the riverbottom near the bank, just under
       the water, spreads photographic papers in them, adjusts it, moves back.
       Watches.

12.   Moonlight sways down through black water onto the photographic
       papers.

13.   She stands by the strobe in deep reeds.

14.   Flash of strobe surprises the riverbank.

15.   She sits awhile in the reeds, arms on knees.

        SUBTITLE: *"Overtakelessness" (what facts lack).*

16.   She is driving, windows blowing, empty highway.

        SUBTITLE: *As usual she enjoyed the sense of work, of having worked.*
                        Other fears would soon return.

"Lots of Guns: An Oratorio for Five Voices" in *Gulf Coast*

"Beckett's Theory of Tragedy"; "Beckett's Theory of Comedy"; "Ode to the Sublime by Monica Vitti"; and "Kant's Question About Monica Vitti" in *London Review of Books*

"Lines"; "Some Afternoons She Does Not Pick Up the Phone"; "Despite Her Pain, Another Day"; "Stanzas, Sexes, Seductions"; "Gnosticisms I, II, III, IV, V, VI" in *The New Yorker*

"No Port Now"; "Nothing For It"; and "Her Beckett" in *The Paris Review*

"Every Exit Is an Entrance (A Praise of Sleep)" in *Prairie Fire*

"Sleepchains"; "Sunday"; "That Strength"; "Methinks the Poor Town Has Been Troubled Too Long"; "Longinus' Dream of Antonioni"; and "And Reason Remains Undaunted" in *Raritan*

"Guillermo's Sigh Symphony" and "Quad" in *Threepenny Review*

ILLUSTRATION CREDITS

Grateful acknowledgment is made to the following for permission to reprint previously published material:

Galerie René Blouin: *Seated Figure with Red Angle (1988)*, by Betty Goodwin. Supplied and reproduced by permission of Galerie René Blouin.

Photofest: Monica Vitti in *Il Deserto Rosso*. Supplied and reproduced by permission of Photofest, Inc.

SWR-Media GmbH: "Samuel Beckett: *Quadrat I & II*." Photograph by Hugo Jehle. Supplied and reproduced by kind permission of Südwestrundfunk, Stuttgart (Germany).